Love @ Work

Love @ Work

100 years of the Industrial Christian Fellowship

Ian Randall, Phil Jump and John Weaver

DARTON · LONGMAN + TODD

First published in 2020 by
Darton, Longman and Todd Ltd
1 Spencer Court
140–142 Wandsworth High Street
London SW18 4JJ

Print book ISBN: 978-1-913657-01-7
eBook ISBN: 978-1-913657-16-1

A catalogue record for this book is available from the British Library.

Phototypeset by Kerrypress, St Albans
Printed and bound by Bell & Bain Ltd, Glasgow

Contents

Foreword

This book tells a remarkable story of change within continuity and continuity within change. On its hundredth anniversary, the Industrial Christian Fellowship (ICF) finds itself at a crossroad, pondering its role and future direction as we enter the third decade of the twenty-first century. As the authors themselves admit at the end of the book, they cannot say what the future holds for ICF. Such existential reflection, however, is nothing new for the organisation and could even be said to characterise its history since its foundation shortly after the First World War. With its present name, it was born of a fusion of two earlier bodies, the Navvy Mission Society founded in 1877 and the Christian Social Union born in 1889. The accounts here of those two bodies and how they came together are not of purely historical interest because it is clear that there has been a continuity of commitment over the decades since those first beginnings, in spite of changes of emphasis and constitution, to ideals of enduring importance.

The title *Love@Work* concisely conveys the essence of ICF's continued intention to achieve a holistic marriage between the world of work and the love of God as shown in the life and mission of Jesus Christ. This is sometimes referred to as 'bringing Sunday into Monday' but the authors rightly insist that what is surely sought is for every day of the week to be imbued with that same spirit of love for God and neighbour. Their use of the '@' no less neatly conveys, quite correctly, that this is not some dream of yesteryear but a thoroughly modern and continuingly urgent endeavour.

Had ICF not responded to the changes in the world around it, had it adhered to rigid formulae and not questioned their continuing relevance, there is little doubt that it would have ceased to exist long ago. Its strength has lain precisely in its ability – if not always initially accompanied by willingness – to adapt and to learn, so as to preach the Gospel afresh in every generation, speaking into the particular aim of uniting the worlds of work and worship into an all-embracing realisation of God's love in action.

Some of the changes in the world around ICF were pioneered in its own work. Whilst it cannot claim exclusive authorship, it seems clear that ICF's early advocacy of decent housing, education, sanitary and health provision for the underprivileged – not to mention its early espousal of environmental concerns – can be seen in the creation of the National Health Service, universal pensions provision and other aspects of modern British society, such as ecological awareness, which we now regard as normal. In that sense, ICF has been a happy victim of its own success. The reality is, however, that much remains and will always remain to be done, if Christian values are to prevail over false gods such as 'the market', whose devotees wrongly claim that it will inevitably lead to a fair society through its own internal self-compensating mechanisms. Experience shows us otherwise.

Friendly critics have insisted that the role of ICF is engagement not academic theorising, although one might argue that the two are complementary and of equal or greater value when combined. The balance between them is something that the organisation will have to work out for itself as it once more adapts to a changing world. The key point here is surely that there is no aspect of the world of work which is out of bounds to the Gospel. From bullying to modern slavery, from non-discriminatory recruitment and career development to something as simple but elusive as equal pay for equal work, from gross disparities in remuneration in companies and institutions to issues such as unfair dismissal, the list is virtually endless. As the authors wryly note, it is curious that some of those seemingly so keen to take Sunday into Monday have shown less enthusiasm in the opposite direction. There is much to do and there always will be. As the history of ICF's story demonstrates so eloquently, the world does not stand still. Those who think it does, get left behind.

The three authors have done a fine job of providing a history, a rationale and glimpse of the potential for ICF's future. Even if ICF has at times felt as though it were a voice crying in the wilderness, it has nonetheless persisted in urging us to make straight the way of the Lord. I commend this book.

+ Justin Welby
Archbishop of Canterbury

Acknowledgements

In telling the story of 100 years of the Industrial Christian Fellowship (ICF), we have made extensive use of the archive of the Fellowship. This is held in the Lambeth Palace Library. We wish to thank the staff of the library for their willing help as we have asked for and consulted many items from the substantial ICF holdings. This rich resource has more still that could be gleaned about the life of the Fellowship.

Another source of material has been the Cambridge University Library (CUL). Among the important publications housed there are the *ICF Quarterly* and the *Faith in Business Quarterly*. The CUL also holds books by key figures in ICF and before that the Navvy Mission Society, such as Elizabeth Garnett and Geoffrey Studdert Kennedy. We thank the CUL staff for their assistance.

Ann Wright, who has been the Secretary of ICF for the past two decades, holds some of the more recent ICF documents and we are most grateful to her.

As we have drafted chapters of this book, we have been indebted to those who have read and commented on what we have written. Our special thanks to Richard Higginson, who has written seminal books in the field of faith and work, and to Anthony Harrop, who brings invaluable expertise from many years with the United Bible Societies. Both have given attention to the historical sections of this book.

In the process of bringing this volume to publication, we have been greatly indebted to David Moloney, the Editorial Director of Darton, Longman and Todd. His own vision is to produce books that are creative and provocative, inspiring and surprising, and the heritage of DLT is inclusive, co-operative, socially aware and spiritually intelligent. We hope that this book will be a worthy introduction to a movement which we believe has exhibited these qualities in its 100-year history.

Ian Randall
Research Associate, Cambridge Centre for Christianity Worldwide

Phil Jump
Regional Minister, North Western Baptist Association and Chair of ICF

John Weaver
Vice President of the John Ray Initiative – connecting Environment, Science and Christianity, and an Executive Committee member of ICF

www.icf-online.org

Introduction

As a young Victorian widow made her way, one autumn afternoon, across the fields and meadows of the Yorkshire Dales, she could hardly imagine that she was taking the first steps in the journey of an organisation that just over a century later would be bringing together government ministers and international business leaders as part of the transformation of British manufacturing. She made her way along a woodland path to the construction site of a nearby reservoir that would soon provide fresh running water to the rapidly expanding urban centres of Leeds and Bradford. Yet her journey was pursued with exactly the same intent that would one day bring captains of industry halfway across the world, as there were two defining realities that they shared in common. The first was that, for each, the scene that confronted them represented the latest advances in industrial expansion. For the Victorians, the rapid development of a transport infrastructure and programme of public works was a defining feature of their era; for those who gathered a century or so later, the increasing partnership between British and Japanese manufacturers was one that transformed, among others, the European car industry. But what also compelled them to make their ground-breaking journeys was a shared conviction that the people of God and the message of the Gospel belong at the very centre of the world that they encountered and the innovations that it generates.

This book is dedicated to telling the story of the intervening years and beyond, as it traces the often-difficult journey of The Industrial Christian Fellowship (ICF) as it evolved from the Navvy Mission Society, amalgamating with the Christian Social Union to eventually become what it is today. But while committed to providing a historical account to mark the 100th year since ICF's formation, we have been determined from the outset that this should be a book about mission. ICF has always existed because of an unstinting belief in the transforming potential of Christian faith. We believe that it can impact the lives of individuals and, through this, influence entire communities for good as they become truly committed to its purpose and cause.

But for this to even begin to become reality requires significant commitment. Firstly, commitment to an understanding of Christian faith that refuses to restrict itself to the confines and cloisters of organised church, but sees itself primarily as defining the nature of society as a whole. In their defence, many leaders of churches in Britain have recognised this to be true, but have often struggled to move beyond the institutional expectations and necessities that have come to define what faith is. As ICF itself bears testimony, there is always a balance to be struck between investing in the front-line vision of an organisation, and investing in the organisation itself, for the sake of it sustaining its cause in future generations. Yet we have to acknowledge that faith can also be perceived as a haven from which to escape the realities of a broken world, and at its worst can numb people into failing to recognise and challenge that brokenness and the causes that underlie it, or indeed the full scope of our vision of the Kingdom of God, which imagines a world that is very different.

This was certainly true of the reality in which Elizabeth Garnett, that young Victorian widow, found herself. Everyone was all too aware of the poor reputation of navvies, whose transient lifestyle took them as labourers from site to site as the great Victorian infrastructure projects began to take shape. As people marvelled at the accomplishments of renowned engineers and entrepreneurs, the Church could at times be no less complicit in ignoring and excluding those whose monotonous and danger-ridden toil brought these things to reality. And it would seem that, while many would lament the navvies' perceived lack of interest in more religious pursuits, they were blind to a reciprocal dismay at their own utter indifference to the appalling and dangerous conditions in which a whole sector of society were forced to labour or starve. It took not only a vision to see things differently but also a relentless commitment to engage with others in an enterprise to advocate and develop an effective response, for that reality to begin to change.

Believing in different
Such endeavours are triggered by what commentators will sometimes describe as a 'holy discontent' that can emerge both from within and without church-related activities. Elizabeth Garnett would be one who

embraced both aspects of this. She had learned from her father, a Church of England clergyman, to be dissatisfied with a Church that was unable to include and cater for the spiritual needs of navvy communities, but she learned from those communities themselves to be dissatisfied with a world in which they were dehumanised, exploited and disadvantaged. At the heart of the Christian Scriptures is a view of humanity that is sacred, crafted in the likeness of its Creator and of ultimate dignity and worth. She could not leave unchallenged a set of social conditions that contradicted this at every turn. This same discontent was echoed in future generations as military chaplains, who had witnessed the violent slaughter of the battlefields of the Western Front, became prophets to a post-war generation in the face of ongoing poverty and inequality. It has since found expression in the face of realities as diverse as race discrimination, climate change, gender inequality, mass unemployment and the emergence of the so-called 'gig economy'. ICF has often shown itself to be an early advocate of the issues of justice that emerge in such contexts and has done so with an ongoing desire to see women and men discover Christian faith for themselves. It has always pursued these aims through a combination of advocacy for those whose voices might otherwise not be heard and rigorous research and theological reflection. Our context may have changed significantly in the intervening years, but we are faced today with a Church in the West that increasingly struggles to attract significant sectors of society, and indeed a society where many remain in situations that are not difficult to describe as dehumanising. The mission of Christ is far from accomplished!

The contemporary theologian Andrew Shanks speaks of a 'solidarity of the shaken'. The term solidarity might easily be re-cast as 'fellowship' and his perception of 'shakenness' is another way of describing the underlying purpose of the particular Fellowship whose story is in view. He borrows the term from the Czech dissident philosopher Jan Patočka, who was one of a number of activists and writers who voiced resistance against the Communist authorities through a movement known as Charter 77. To be shaken is to be both subjected to the traumas that a dysfunctional society can generate and stirred from the complacency of simply accepting that 'this is the way things are'. There are those within every culture, both victims and beneficiaries of its inequalities and injustices, who will not stop to question these perpetual wrongs, or indeed the structures and systems that generate them. At the very least, ICF has seen itself as one of those voices through which such people might be stirred and shaken into a different consciousness; at its most ambitious, as nothing less than commissioned to lead the building of the alternative society that such voices demand. Shanks describes the current climate as one of unprecedented opportunity for society to recognise 'the actual truth of God'.

It is possibilities like these that have motivated us to put this story together: for whatever the future might have in store for ICF, the vision that brought it into being and the Gospel imperative that undergirded it are undiminished. It has often been a challenging road, both through the personal fragility of those who carried this message – a significant number of ICF's principal advocates seem to have died at a relatively young age – but also because of the inherent difficulties it entails. The Fellowship has always sought to hold two core principles together: seeking social change in the context of advocating personal allegiance to Christ, and always commending a vision of the Gospel that impacts the whole of life to those who express such allegiance. And it has always sought to do so through a combination of informed research and practical intervention. It has often been criticised for pursuing one at the expense of another; in its time, the religious have accused the Fellowship of being too political, activists have complained that it is too academic, while others have been wary of its overt commitment to active Christianity. This sadly evidences a prevailing view that these are somehow in opposition, and we would argue that effective mission needs always to embrace them as belonging together.

In reality, ICF has often paid a heavy price for refusing to be the very thing of which its critics accused it. Had it chosen to pursue one of these avenues at the expense of the others, perhaps it might now be as significant a player in wider society as the Labour Party or Trades Union Congress, or an influential department or publishing house within the confines of organised Christianity or academia. But it has insisted that these worlds need to come together as a greater whole, and has concentrated its efforts in those places where the gaps appear rather than the safe havens that one or other of these offer in isolation.

Yet this is not something for which those institutions should take the blame entirely, for we exist in a society that has all too often preferred the message of the Church to be contained within the relative safety of a private faith expressed through religious ritual and institution. The Jesus who was prepared to overturn the tables of exploitative market traders and incur the wrath of governing authorities is one whose message will always disturb those whose interests are served by the wrongs in society remaining unrighted. ICF's story is one of faithful commitment to those values that first took Elizabeth Garnett on a life-changing journey across the Yorkshire Dales. As we look back, it is hard to avoid a measure of dismay not only at the way those principles have been unheeded by wider society, but also that many of ICF's prophetic warnings have become realised. It cannot be denied that, in the subsequent years, the Christian community has provided a number of well-presented and carefully researched critiques of prevailing issues, nor have these been entirely ignored, but it remains perceived more as a moral commentator than the architect of an alternative reality in the here and now. We write in an age where postmodernism is challenging many of the established assumptions on which contemporary society is founded, and can do so therefore, with a degree of optimism, not only because ICF had long-since recognised that many of these were less than they claimed, but as Andrew Shanks anticipates, there might yet emerge an arena in which its voice can be recognised and heeded.

The power of love

It may seem strange that we should depict such an account as one of love, for this is a narrative that could hardly be described as romantic. Yet this perhaps underlines something of that same dilemma. Our concept of love, as something that represents mere emotion and affection, is a similar attempt to disempower and caricature a reality whose true place is one of defining the very nature of society and commerce. This is a story that is lived out in the brutal environment of navvy camps, inner-city tenements and factory floors, the forensic debating chambers of leading universities, the blood-stained battlefields of two world wars, and the gruelling confrontations between unionised labour and company directors. In this respect, it is anything but a romance, yet it speaks of those who were compelled to engage themselves at the very heart of these realities through a far deeper and more profound understanding of the love of God.

It was love for the navvies that led Elizabeth Garnett to become such an ardent advocate for their cause. It was a love for those whose lives and bodies were shattered by both industrial warfare and the appalling deprivation of Britain's industrial urban centres that caused Geoffrey Studdert Kennedy, ICF's 'Special Messenger' in the 1920s, to quite literally work himself to death in their service. But it was also a love for God and a recognition of the transforming power of that love that spurred their efforts forward. The Old Testament book of Deuteronomy contains one of the most wide-ranging visions of a society that is defined by the goodness and justice of

God. Its law-codes set themselves in direct contrast to the life of slavery and enforced labour from which the Israelite people had been liberated. In so doing, it acknowledges industrial operations at their worst, but conveys a positive and compelling alternative. This is one where provision is made for the disadvantaged, burdensome debt is curtailed, communal rather than personal wealth is commended, justice is universally available and God's concerns are portrayed as extending even to issues of public health with the provision of appropriate sanitation. Yet all of these are heralded as exemplifying love; the practical outworking of a society whose members are defined by a call to 'love the Lord your God' with every ounce of their being. We should be no less surprised therefore that, in the second decade of the twenty-first century, ICF found itself working with the Winchester Business School to explore the place of love in contemporary business practice, as inherited models of management theory became increasingly discredited and exposed as ethically inadequate. And to underline this reality, even as this publication was undergoing its final stages of editing, in a letter to the current Chair, ICF veteran John Davis observed:

> All kinds of work must be performed with love to be pleasing to God. I think 'working with love' is most meaningful when we work 'inspired by the Spirit of love', work that is guided, helped and empowered by God.

But this has always been a two-way conversation. It is all too easy for well-intentioned Christians to lose sight of the love of God in their enthusiasm for mission. Narratives and theories of Christian mission can all too often resemble the marketing strategies of the corporate world, with a bottom line of 'bums on seats' often expressed in an arena of competition and organisational success. The worst outcomes of this were particularly highlighted at a conference in 2019 at which ICF was represented by its Chair. The gathering was invited to review the fruits of David Clark's Kingdom at Work project and in particular to consider how the identified principles of the Kingdom of God might be offered as a tool for managers and directors to construct a workplace culture of wellbeing. In affirming the project's potential, participants could not help but observe that the environment they envisaged was one that could be seen as starkly absent in some local church contexts.

True participation in the mission of God will seldom take place without significant sacrifice, and through its pages, this book also seeks to pay tribute to many who have engaged in the work of ICF, often at great personal cost. Love is costly, and many of ICF's most effective advocates recognised that the change in society and in people's lives, for which they yearned, could only be realised if they were willing for this to impact their own life circumstances. Elizabeth Garnett quite literally took on the identity of a navvy – her 'mates' as she often described them – and ICF could at times be quite uncompromising in its expectations of those it recruited as missioners. Their story may go some way to inspiring others to follow in their wake, but their sacrifice is testimony to a ministry defined by the love of God. We would maintain that the key motivator for Christian mission must always be a profound appreciation of the nature and extent of this divine love. It is this, over and above the interests of any religious institution, that we should seek to exemplify in our contemporary endeavours. The mission of God, however else it might be expressed, should always be recognisable as 'love at work'.

Telling love's story

There is no denying that many of the key concerns that ICF worked hard to express have found their way into subsequent legislation and become part of our everyday life. It is now unthinkable that many of the social ills that its early advocates were so keen to eradicate would be tolerated in contemporary society; this is not to say that they no longer exist, but when they emerge, they are at least accompanied by an appropriate chorus of instinctive outrage. Yet perhaps it is this apparent success that has made ICF's task increasingly difficult as the years have gone by, for its aim, as it often clearly contended, was never to construct some kind of utopia inspired by religious virtue, but to see this as the natural consequence of individual members of society apprehending the all-encompassing love of God. For all that these things matter, we seem to have developed a world view where they are perceived as the responsibilities of legislators, and we are almost as outraged when local communities take initiative in the absence of government intervention, as we are by such realities existing in the first place. ICF finds itself in a context today where social reform is perceived as evidence of the virtue of the state rather than a shared expression of Christian values and identity.

How then do we communicate the love of God? This has to remain one of the foundational questions for those who believe themselves to be commissioned by Christ to engage their contemporary world as advocates of the Gospel. This is a world that is becoming less and less separated by geographic distance, yet more and more defined by social, economic and technological inequality. The call to 'go into all the world' is as much one that requires intention and effort to engage with every strata and subculture of the society that surrounds us, as it does to travel to any distant shore. Work is a social as well as an economic activity; it has the power to reinforce the divisions of society or to become a place where they are overcome through common endeavour and creativity. It is in the world of work, either through deliberate exploitation or unintended neglect, that injustice and inequality can be perpetuated and accelerated, and through work that they can be exposed and combatted. God's love for humanity requires his followers to seek justice and to love mercy – to pursue this without any engagement in the world of work is to condemn ourselves to fail before it has even begun. To love God is to love the world as God loves the world; for that love to be tangibly demonstrated, it needs to be made known in the workplaces of every society. For it is here that humanity is to be found, and here that humanity has the potential to do its best or its worst. Its leaders, its ministers of state, its entrepreneurs, its role models become what they are through being at work, and through work shape the society in which we live, move and have our being. If this is to be a society that is defined by the love of God, then it can only be so if God's love is expressed and articulated within that environment where opinion is formed and policy developed. God's love needs to be made known in and through the world of work, whether we engage as clients, customers or employees.

Yet the great visions of state will never become reality unless these have widespread and popular assent, unless the collective endeavours of the population can be harnessed in the same common accord. For God's love to be known and experienced in society as a whole means that God's love must be experienced either through personal encounter or by participation in a community of which it is an expression. If faith and work are not in harmony, then not only is our world less than God's ideal but faith will not make sense to those whose identity is significantly defined, for good or ill, by the work that they do. The work of the cross, expressed by the writer of Colossians in the New Testament, is to reconcile all things (Colossians 1:20): to address the fractures and fault lines where God's purposes and human intent have become misaligned. To engage in the mission of God is a calling to become part of that ministry of reconciliation. The world of work is both our mission field and the measure of our success.

Like the writer of Deuteronomy, there was a day when ICF saw its role as the architect of that society. It stood ready to build those economic and social structures that could be the agents of God's reconciliation. With time it proved itself an able influencer, but often at the expense of its own sustainability. Today its vision is no less ambitious but its practice is on a far smaller scale. Where those fractures and fault lines are detected, and the capacity and intent to be reconcilers exist, ICF has sought to be an active supporter and enabler. It seeks to offer the fruits of its work and partnership as faithful symbols of the world it believes in – faithful symbols of God's love that are meaningful to the context that has shaped them. It takes its place alongside every other agent of God's mission in our contemporary world, often engaged in quite different and distinct projects and endeavours but bound by a common call. This is a call to create signs and expressions of God's love and reconciliation in the language and symbols that make sense in the situation from which they have emerged. We offer the lessons we have learned, the successes and failures that make up our story, as a resource to those who share our commitment to God's mission purpose.

Yet if this is to remain rooted in the love of God, it must be rooted in the worship of God, and throughout its history, ICF has made no excuse for being an explicitly prayerful and sacramental organisation. It is fascinating to note how so many of its keenest activists have also been those who might be described as being inclined to a High Church tradition. As we will go on to discover, the early founders of the Christian Social Union saw the Eucharist as central to their common identity. This to them was a sign of the solidarity that they desired for all of humanity. Later, through the writings of Studdert Kennedy, it was the sacrifice of the cross, represented and experienced in the bread and wine of the altar, that enabled him to connect the inescapable human suffering that confronted him with the narratives of his faith. Some years later, when ICF launched a series of theme pamphlets, the inaugural publication was entitled *He Took Bread* – remembering that the bread and wine, brought to the table of communion, are the outcome of human endeavour. In this most significant act of Christian worship, the outpoured love of God and the work of human hands are brought together.

Yet for all of this, those who seemed so at home in the High Church rituals of the Anglo-Catholic tradition, through the ministry of ICF were also staunch advocates of a sustained and intentional endeavour to seek the personal conversion of the workforce of Britain. They acted and spoke with an evangelistic zeal that many contemporary evangelicals would struggle to match. To some degree, we might argue that this was a product of its time, and that the assumed distinction between these two traditions is not as profound as some claim. But perhaps it is also a testament to an organisation that refused to be contained by any religious tradition in its desire to affirm 'Christ the Lord of all life'.

So this is the story of a Mission that joined a Union to become a Fellowship. The book itself is the outcome of a collaboration that has emerged as the narrative has been put together. Phil Jump, present Chair of ICF, has sought to reflect missionally on the various episodes in the organisation's life and particularly explore the wider contexts in which it was operating. John Weaver has sought to develop some of the theological issues that this raises. But neither could have attempted this if it had not been for the patient endeavours of Ian Randall, whose research and historical expertise first brought the story together. All of us share a deep commitment to Christian mission and seek to be faithful ministers of the Gospel. We all have an interest in church and social history and have found ourselves intrigued by the particular history of ICF and some of the characters that emerge from it. We make this point to underline the fact that we see these three elements as belonging together. As we seek to encourage others to engage in the mission of God, we hope that they will share this conviction. Christian mission is above all else the work of God and, without an informed commitment to understanding the nature and purpose of God, it risks becoming little more than religious marketing. Missional enterprise that ignores the potential lessons of history will at best hamper itself by repeating them and at worst be destined to fail from the outset. It is for this reason that we unapologetically offer a historical narrative in the context and for the purposes of contemporary mission.

As a way of structuring that, we have sought through each chapter, alongside the historical narrative, to introduce and explore a particular approach to mission that we perceive as somehow reflected in the story that is told. This is not to say that the same issues do not emerge in other eras, and indeed there is a fair degree of unavoidable overlap. This is to be expected, as we wanted the story to define its own narrative and not be forced into the mould of an imposed structure. Chapter 1 particularly highlights the current trends towards Fresh Expressions and Whole-Life Discipleship. These might be perceived as relatively recent innovations, but we can note that the work of the two organisations whose amalgamation created ICF were an early representation of each of these. Their work was largely developed at the turn of the nineteenth and twentieth centuries. Chapter 2 particularly seeks to focus on the Church's calling to be a prophetic presence in society. Through the story of ICF's early formation, it highlights the tension between maintaining effective channels of influence and remaining true to our message at the risk of not being heard. Chapter 3 is the only one that is largely devoted to a single personality, Geoffrey Studdert Kennedy, who is arguably the individual who most personifies the very essence of what ICF believes itself called to be. We focus on him as a pioneer, another term that enjoys significant contemporary attention, recognising the inevitable tensions that can sometimes exist between innovator and organisation and the vital role of those who can build appropriate structures of support around pioneers. Yet we cannot avoid the tragic reality that individuals with such a 'driven' personality will always run the risk of sacrificing too much of their own wellbeing in pursuit of their cause.

We continue in Chapter 4 to trace the inevitable struggles that any organisation will face as its founding personalities pass on the baton to successive generations. This can often be a moment where the demands of the organisation become as consuming as the vision around which it was formed. Though it might feel like something of a paradox, Chapter 5 could be described as outlining the cost of success. While Christian mission might express itself as founded in Christ, its purpose will often be conveyed in tangible outcomes that can, quite reasonably, become an end in themselves. How do we cope when the world at large sees our material successes as being of greater significance than the one in whose name they were initiated? How do we avoid becoming victim of a media that can laud our achievements while playing down – if not deliberately obscuring – our Christian identity? Chapter 6 particularly explores the challenges and opportunities that emerge when the landscape in which we are operating begins to change. It highlights the importance of learning to re-cast our defining vision in the light of this. Chapter 7 acknowledges the cost of innovation and raises a dilemma, which many visionaries will face – to what degree is it right to persuade and motivate others to rise to the challenge of a large-scale initiative, and to what degree should our ambition be tempered by the resources that are available to us? Is it better to have tried and failed, or is it better to remain to fight another day? The final chapter particularly seeks to explore the role of partnership, perhaps at times embraced through necessity of scale, but also because it epitomises much of how contemporary innovation and enterprise tends to operate.

Learning love's lessons
But these are lessons that ICF also has to learn. We notice that, at many of the key watersheds in the life of the organisation, some form of

reflective history has been put together as the basis for moving forward. As ICF reaches its centenary, there are serious questions that need to be asked about its future direction, if indeed there remains a role for it as an organisation in its own right. ICF exists today because it has always been willing to embrace change and to re-form itself around new realities. Yet, in so doing, it always retained a clear sense of its overarching purpose and the vision that it is called to carry forward into the next phase of its existence. In the pages that follow, we hope not only to underline that reality but also to draw out that vision and purpose for our future context. We recognise that relatively few people might have encountered The Industrial Christian Fellowship as a distinct organisation, but we offer our story, because we believe that many will recognise and celebrate some of the innovations and developments that it has helped to initiate. Some might even be surprised to discover that ICF is part of their own story. But anyone who is a trade unionist, a beneficiary of the welfare state, has appreciated the ministry of a chaplain or has read their health and safety policy at work, to mention but a few, can thank The Industrial Christian Fellowship. Those who made up its membership will have played some part in their evolution. Anyone who believes in the transforming potential of God's love and the need for it to find tangible expression in their contemporary experience has something to learn from the story we tell.

On the borders of Merseyside and West Lancashire, there is a statue that is known as the Halsall Navvy. Its stands near a popular gastro pub on the banks of the Leeds and Liverpool Canal. It depicts the upper body of a muscle-bound man, shovel in hand, almost bursting from the ground, and claims to mark the spot where the first earth was dug out in the waterway's construction. The canal has long since ceased to be an industrial highway and is now perceived as a haven for wildlife, walkers, anglers, leisure craft and casual diners. Its presence is taken for granted as a long-standing feature of the local landscape, and many will struggle to imagine that it hasn't always be there. The Halsall Navvy, a relatively recent installation, refuses to allow this history to remain forgotten any longer. He demands that passers-by recognise the graft and toil that brought this now idyllic canal into existence; he seeks in a small way to right the wrongs of a culture that was happy to ignore him and the appalling deprivation and exploitation that canal-building entailed. The Halsall Navvy has broken out of the forgotten ground, bursting to the surface in a pile of earth that a couple of centuries ago was being literally put in place by his forebears. Perhaps this publication serves a similar purpose. Much of ICF's endeavour has been hidden; many of those who sought to implement its vision were perceived by wider society as acting in a different capacity; many of its ideas were taken forward and attributed to other organisations. But through this publication, we hope that some of ICF's story can once again manage to break through to the surface and be recognised for the part it played in constructing what might often today be taken for granted.

As we began to envisage the production of this book, the emerging political narratives indicated that ICF's centenary was increasingly likely to coincide with the year that marked Britain's formal departure from the European Union. It was easy to see the resonances between this and those key moments after two world wars when, for different reasons, there was a need to redefine the principles and values that would determine the society that emerged. This seemed an opportune moment for the ground to be broken and its story to emerge. This was a point in wider history where we might all benefit from being reminded again of the role that ICF had sought to play at those previous watershed moments. More importantly, it was a moment to re-hear some of the significant messages of which ICF has been the bearer. In reality, much of the final editing and composition has taken place in a previously unimagined world, where issues about European identity have been eclipsed by a worldwide pandemic of COVID-19. Those who have put this manuscript together have worked as a 'solidarity of the shaken', living in lockdown, recognising their own vulnerability. Yet we also find ourselves compelled to ask questions about how our world became what it now is, and recognising that, in even more dramatic ways, significant questions will be asked about the nature of our future.

And so we offer our story as one that might inform those who are already asking similar things, and to those who are not, in the hope it might cause such questions to emerge.

Chapter 1

Forerunners of the Fellowship

Two key features of the emerging Christian landscape in the early decades of a new millennium are Whole-Life Discipleship and Fresh Expressions. The former refers to a recognition that effective Christianity is not simply a matter of regular participation in the institutions and activities of the Church, but also includes embedding the values, behaviours and narratives of our faith in the everyday activities of life and work. The latter recognises the vital benefits of Christian community, but acknowledges that a fair amount of what we describe as 'church-life' is a cultural remnant of the age in which our congregations were founded. While continuing to value these, there is a growing recognition of a pressing need to find ways of shaping and sustaining Christian communities that are relevant to the lifestyles and cultures of those who are not attracted by our traditional activities.

These two aspects of being church demand significant attention from those who are serious about mission today. They also interrelate. Fresh Expressions are founded on an appreciation of the 24/7 lifestyle of those they seek to reach and are open to being shaped by it. In so doing they stimulate and inform Christian discipleship within that context.

Those concerned to explore such issues might not be inclined to study the history of a movement that has reached its centenary at the same time as they are being envisioned. But in the case of The Industrial Christian Fellowship (ICF), its early history could be described as the coming together of two earlier organisations that in their own ways sought to embody exactly these principles of 24/7 discipleship and a lived faith beyond traditional Sunday services.

Those two organisations are the Navvy Mission Society (NMS), formed in 1877, which had as its focus the needs of labourers in public works – the navvies – and the Christian Social Union (CSU), formed in 1889, which concentrated more on Christian social thinking. They might not have described themselves as such, but the Navvy Mission existed to develop expressions of church-life in what was otherwise a forgotten and neglected sector of society, while the Christian Social Union increasingly recognised that, while Christian values might have been effectively communicated within the institutions of the Church, they were glaringly absent in many aspects of the society of which it was a part. The simple truth was that many of those who faithfully attended the churches and chapels on Sunday, at the same time perpetuated and tolerated social conditions from Monday to Saturday which contradicted much of what their faith stood for. CSU sought to challenge that reality.

These two organisations were – not surprisingly – very different in their composition and aims, and part of the genius of ICF was the way in which it blended them together. This chapter looks at these two forerunners of the Fellowship and how they became one movement in 1920. This early period is often associated with the dynamic figure of Geoffrey Studdert Kennedy, or 'Woodbine Willie', and he was certainly of far-reaching significance, but there is a great deal more to the ICF story. The antecedents are vital in understanding what the organisation was seeking to achieve and, in tracing their story, there are some vital lessons to be learned for Christian mission in any era.

Concern for navvies

The nineteenth century was one of immense expansion of infrastructure and public works in Britain, and a good deal of the associated earthworks were physically dug out by teams of labourers more commonly called navvies. The term 'navvy' came from a shortening of 'navigator', and was initially attached to those tasked with digging out the course of the canal systems. The term was subsequently extended to manual labourers working on railways, tunnels, drainage and sewage systems, bridges, and dams.

The number of navvies in Britain was at one time comparable to an army. About 30 per cent were Irish. Navvies needed to move from place to place, which contributed to their being outsiders who experienced significant social isolation. Navvies had their own settlements, usually composed of wooden shacks lacking basic amenities, and were inevitably transitory. For most people, navvies were an 'underclass', ranking below the working classes, and they were despised and feared. Rates of accident and death were higher among navvies than among any other group in Britain. While fatalities often took place as a result of unsafe working conditions, there was also a high incidence of death because of outbreaks of typhus, cholera and dysentery as well as because of heavy drinking. As will be seen, however, those who took the trouble to get to know this community found that there was much more to them than the common perception.

There were various attempts by Christian groups and individuals to reach navvies, especially those working on railway construction, before the Navvy Mission Society was formed. This was typical of the way in which entrepreneurial figures initiated outreach to many different groups in society in the Victorian era. Thomas Fayers, for example, was a railway missionary and wrote a book in 1858 about his experiences, *Labour Among the Navvies*. But these various outreach activities were not initially co-ordinated. The beginning of the NMS is connected with the building of the Lindley Wood Reservoir, which was being constructed in the Washburn valley, north of Otley, Yorkshire, for Leeds Corporation. Navvies worked on this scheme between 1869 and 1876. In the autumn of 1871, a 32-year-old widow, Elizabeth Garnett, who was to become the principal figure in the NMS, visited the Washburn valley at a time when there was an outbreak of typhoid within the camp. The story of Elizabeth Garnett is sometimes told as if she discovered the lives of the navvies for the first time on this visit. The reality is that she had known for years about the brutal conditions under which they worked.

Elizabeth Hart, later Garnett, was born in 1839, the daughter of Joshua and Hannah Hart. Her father was the Vicar of Otley and as a parish minister he was concerned for the men working on the nearby Bramhope Tunnel and Arthington Viaduct for the Leeds to Thirsk railway. In July 1846, 400 of these men walked to Otley Parish Church for the funeral of a fellow worker who had died on his first day at work. Deaths of those engaged in such work were frequent. As well as the evident dangers of the work, as in the case of this fatality, navvies worked long hours and were very poorly nourished – which had serious effects on their health and welfare. In 1849, a Navvies Memorial mausoleum was built near the Otley vicarage as a reminder of their loss of life. Elizabeth Hart married a young clergyman, Charles Garnett, in 1862, but she suffered a tragic loss herself when Charles died within a year of their marriage.

In 1872, Elizabeth embarked on what would be a lifetime of work with navvies and their families. She opened a Sunday school at the Lindley Wood site and decided to set up home in the Washburn valley. She was to live there, in a room, for four years. Her move was strongly opposed by friends, some of whom said navvies were 'not fit for any lady with right feeling to go amongst'. They had a reputation for hard drinking sprees, prize-fights and gambling. Many had little if any time for clergymen. But a somewhat different perception was emerging in the 1870s. Katie Marsh, who like Elizabeth was the daughter of a clergyman, met some of the navvies from Crystal Palace, London, in 1853. When she got to know some of them better, since they were lodging near where she lived in Beckenham, then a Kent country village, she found them rather different from the drunkards and brawlers portrayed in the press. Her experience was that many were warm, friendly men, often shy at first in dealings with strangers, since they had normal relationships with so few outside their own community.

The impact of her book about them, *English Hearts and English Hands: Or, the Railway and the Trenches* (1858), was considerable. For many, such as Aggie Weston, who founded the Sailors' Homes, it was inspirational. The same concern that Elizabeth Garnett felt for the Lindley Wood navvies had already been felt by Lewis Moule Evans, a young Anglican clergyman. After being a curate in Otley, he became the Rector of nearby Leathley, and he was prompted to take action. Evans became involved at Lindley Wood, where he encouraged Garnett's involvement. Many Anglican clergymen who attempted to engage with navvy communities often provoked an adverse reaction, which could end up with rough scenes and with the clergymen leaving with bloodied noses. But Evans, like Joshua Hart, found ways of overcoming the antagonism that was often generated. Garnett and Evans gathered information about the public works schemes employing navvies: the number of men, whether there was educational provision (most navvies were illiterate) and what church contact there was, if any. From the results, Evans estimated there were about 40,000 navvies in England. Including women and children, that probably meant a total of around 60,000 people. Only in three instances (as far as could be discovered) out of 72 was there a day school and only one site had a Sunday school.

It is hard to avoid the question of why Elizabeth Garnett and her associates succeeded in an area where so many others had failed. It does not feel insignificant that such a high proportion of this foundational work was undertaken by women, particularly given the patriarchal nature of Victorian society and the 'macho' culture that seemed to prevail within navvy communities. Their story has much to teach us about the effectiveness of approaches to mission that are able to subvert rather than confront the prevailing structures that stand against them. Is it more than irony that a social class who had become largely overlooked and marginalised were reached by those whose gender often attracted a similar reaction?

But there seems another element present within Garnett's approach that stands in contrast to some of those earlier failed efforts. Within her writings and actions, we can detect a genuine recognition of the worth and dignity of the navvy community rather than merely a concern at their absence from the regular activities and institutions of an existing Church. At that Otley funeral, in those 400 mourners and the tragic death of their colleague, she glimpsed a momentary expression of humanity, before they once again dissolved into a faceless commodity to be valued only by the amount of earth they could shift in a day.

Rather than asking herself why this mass of souls was not present to swell the congregation on normal Sundays, she seemed more concerned with why the Church had only managed to become present for them in death. To what degree was their non-participation due more to a lack of opportunity than inclination? It was this that led her, literally and metaphorically, to make her dwelling among them and develop an expression of mission from within. She became an advocate in wider society for their cause and so earned the right to become an advocate for the Gospel in theirs.

A Navvy Mission: steps taken

This was also the principle that Lewis Moule Evans adopted and, in the winter of 1874–75, he prepared an article, 'Navvies and Their Needs', for one of the many religious weeklies of the time, *The Quiver*, asking for help in setting up a Mission to their community. He followed this with a leaflet, also called *Navvies and Their Needs*, which set out clearly their situation:

> Navvies form a class by themselves, isolated: first, by the nature of their work, which is often carried on in places remote from towns or even villages; secondly by their roving habits; and thirdly by the belief, which commonly prevails among them, that they are looked upon as outcasts.

He argued that specially framed mission work was needed. This was already beginning to happen at Lindley Wood, and before the work there finished a Christian Excavators' Union was formed, with 25 navvy members and eight others.

Towards the end of 1877, Evans followed his article and leaflet with 4,000 printed appeals and a similar number of letters that were written and sent to a range of people. Within a remarkably short period, substantial sums of money came in and Evans was able to set up his new society. Evans himself was the first Secretary of the Navvy Mission Society and Robert

Bickersteth, the Bishop of Ripon, became its President. Evans' health was deteriorating – he had tuberculosis – but in the summer of 1878 he was able to visit workers at the dams at Cheltenham, Denshaw, Fewston, and Barden Moor, and in the early autumn he made the sea-crossing to the Isle of Man Railway works. He was able to appoint seven local lay missionaries around the country, a remarkable achievement in the space of a few months. Evans died suddenly early in December 1878, at the age of thirty-two, and was buried in the Leathley graveyard. Navvies attended his funeral to pay their respects.

Elizabeth Garnett then stepped in to give leadership to the infant Society. The early focus was on seeking to appoint lay missionaries (preferably but not exclusively ex-navvies) to provide mission rooms, and – if possible – to establish night schools where navvies could learn to read and write. The vision for education was wide in scope: it envisaged libraries being established at each centre of public works where navvies were employed. Considering the transitory nature of these sites, this was a remarkable ambition, but gradually they were established. The books were of a general educational nature, including books on science. Geology was one of the popular subjects, which intrigued some later writers. But this was not surprising given the connection of navvies with the earth and the fact that William Smith (1769–1839), the 'father of English geology', drew maps of the geology of England and Wales based on what he observed in the construction of the canal system and coal mining. Books with specifically spiritual content were also included. As interest grew, a standard scheme emerged of site-based libraries with 250 books each.

Much of the initial work of the Mission was carried out without the backing of the building contractors, engineers and city corporations. Elizabeth Garnett later recalled conversations in which – for example – an engineer stated that in the evenings, after work, the navvies should be in bed and they were 'better without reading'. Very often the contractors refused the Society any building for a day school, even though a friend of the Society undertook to cover all the costs. Existing schools in the vicinity of public works generally refused to admit the children of navvies. When the first NMS school was established and approved by the Government, the education was so effective that 90 per cent of the children passed the government tests which were beginning to be provided to try to create uniform standards in schools.

Mission workers and supporters

As the Mission grew, it attracted voluntary workers, many of them women, who gave a considerable amount of their time to the work. The early experiences of Katherine Sleight were quite typical. She was a widow, with private means, and became involved in the work of the Mission when the Hull–Barnsley railway came near her home. Work was halted in 1884 because of a cash crisis and those navvies who stayed on in the area were left without work and began, with their families, to suffer hunger and malnutrition. The NMS set up a distress fund: Katherine Sleight and a committee of gangers used the money that was raised to purchase basic food for the Hull families and also provided men with money to travel to look for work elsewhere. When Katherine's own money ran out, she took a paid post as the Mission's Association Secretary in London. She was a gifted administrator and fundraiser but she sadly died prematurely (aged forty-six) in 1898.

The Mission was keen to enlist a significant band of supporters who would help to bring its work to the attention of the wider public. Those who became patrons and supporters included the Archbishops of Canterbury and of York, a considerable number of Church of England bishops, and a range of individuals connected with the English aristocracy. The presence of women was crucial, both in the demanding central organisation and in enabling effective local outreach. It remained the case throughout the history of the NMS that their contribution was significant. This affirmation of the leadership of women was not matched, however, by the inclusion of navvies in a similar role. They could be missionaries, and were valued as such, but no navvy was represented in any central Mission Society decisions that were made. From 1893, the Mission had a permanent office in the cellar of the Church of England's Church House, London. The central office paid a third of the costs of local mission initiatives and a third of each missionary's wages – in the 1880s the missionaries received about £80 per year. The rest of the money needed was raised by local Navvy Mission groups.

The Mission's work and the pressing needs of navvies were communicated in various ways. In 1877, Elizabeth Garnett wrote a novel, *Little Rainbow*, which was the story of a boy in a navvy settlement, and she followed that with a number of other books. There was a *Quarterly Letter to Men on Public Works*, distributed free to all navvies, and its contents included items that were intended to relate to their families. This publication lasted in this form from 1879 until 1917, though subsequent editions were produced after ICF was formed. As well as going to navvies, the *Quarterly Letter* also went to supporters of the Mission and through this means money was raised. As time went on, and more money was given, not only were the wages paid to lay missionaries working for the Mission increased, but pensions were also provided for some older retired navvies. In 1906, 146 of these were being paid out. This was a relatively small number compared with the total number of navvies, but it was a noteworthy new development.

The story of David Smith illustrates the lives of the navvy missionaries. He was born in 1866 in Sussex, where his father was a blacksmith. The family moved to Bristol, where his father worked on the docks, and David joined him. David became a committed Christian and in the 1890s an enthusiast for sharing his faith within his workplace. Through this he came to work closely with Robert Grimston, a Chaplain to public works who was to become the Navvy Mission's Secretary. Navvy Smith, as he came to be known, became well known on the Great Central Railway, which ran from Nottingham to London. For a time, he was in charge of the Bulwell Navvy Hut, north of Nottingham. The Hut was actually a house, with a sign which said: 'The Navvy Mission Good Samaritan Home. One Night's Free Lodgings – Given Only To Navvies In Tramp.' He later led missions in various places, including the Catcleugh dam in Northumberland, the Privett tunnel in Hampshire, Shirehampton docks and finally in Birmingham, where he established links with business leaders.

Mission developments over time

While there were changes in the Society's operations from the 1870s to the early twentieth century, Elizabeth Garnett was something of a constant. She died in 1921. To many, she was the embodiment of the Mission. For her, navvies were 'mates', and she called herself a 'navvy'. In 1898, she spoke of how, for many years, she was 'the *unpaid* clerk, Librarian, Editor, Drawing Room Speaker, etc, besides being one of the Committee and Managers of the Society'. She continued: 'I have never been paid *one penny*, and if ever I get so poor that I have to be paid, it will be "good-bye" and you will not see me again. No, I will work for the love of Christ, and for the love of you, or *not at all*.' By that time, a typical centre where the Mission operated had a missionary (in 1891 there were 39 of these) who, as well as being a preacher and pastor, often ran other enterprises: clubs and savings schemes, a mission room with a wooden pulpit and pews and a harmonium, a library, a room to smoke and read in, a school for children, opportunities for training in areas such as first aid, and events such as concerts.

A picture of developments in a local Mission in the early twentieth century can be gained from the story of the Embsay Reservoir, which was built near Skipton, Yorkshire. In June 1906, the Mission's *Quarterly Letter* reported that a missionary, J. R. King, was in place near the reservoir, living in local accommodation, although it seems that King moved on after a few months and was followed by another missionary who spent only a short time at Embsay. The Mission was based in a mill that provided a meeting space for 150 labourers and also living accommodation. The transformation of the mill was so dramatic that it led to it being called a 'mansion'. Regular Sunday services became established, and it appears that these continued even when a missionary was not present. In 1908, the *Quarterly Letter* reported on life at Embsay. A horse driver, known as Scotch Bob, who had suffered an accident at work, had been in hospital where he had had his leg amputated below the knee. He was out of hospital and was 'doing well'. Attention was paid by the Mission to the needs of such individuals.

Although the Embsay experiences give some insights, in other locations – especially where NMS missionaries stayed longer – it was possible to accomplish more. There were some examples of centres where formalised adult education was developed: there were Mission-funded night schools functioning for adults – navvies and their wives – and in a few instances there could be more than one such school in a settlement. However, navvies were often exhausted at the end of the day. Day schools for children were more common and that provision could also be of benefit to wives. In 1906, at the Angram Reservoir, near Harrogate, North Yorkshire, the Mission was even able to raise enough funds to set up a hospital on the site, with a resident nurse and doctor. The good reputation of the Mission had also spread internationally by this time. Its vision for ministry to navvies inspired similar work in several countries, including Canada, New Zealand, Australia, South Africa and Hong Kong.

The impact of the NMS was wide-ranging over time. Christian conversions took place, with consequent changed lives. The police spoke of crime levels dropping when the Mission's workers became involved. Indeed, the Mayor of Ludlow estimated that police court cases reduced by two-thirds when the NMS opened on the Elan pipe track. Living and working conditions were improved, at least in part because of the influence of the Mission, and educational opportunities were significant.

The First World War was a period of change for navvies. Much of the construction work started in the Victorian era had been completed.

Navvies were recruited for the armed forces. After the First World War, Navvy Smith commented:

> The navvy is a far more sober man today; he is better dressed, better educated, takes a keener interest in his social wellbeing and enjoys a status in human society which he never thought of years ago. Who will deny that this is the outcome of Christianity and Labour marching hand in hand?

The reference to Labour alongside Christianity is significant. The NMS decided in 1918, under the Mission's Chairman, Henry H. Pereira, Bishop of Croydon, that it needed to engage with post-war 'reconstruction' and with the 'Labour world'. This was to lead in the following year to a change of name to the The Industrial Christian Fellowship and in 1920 to a move to give more time to social questions through merging with the Christian Social Union.

The formation of the Christian Social Union

The cloisters and spires of Oxford must have seemed a far cry from the navvy camps of the railways, canals and public works, but it was here that this second strand of ICF's identity was beginning to form. While the Navvy Mission Society and many other Victorian organisations were involved in a front-line response to those in need, others – the Christian Social Union (CSU) being the most influential – were encouraging the academic world to consider why these social issues existed in the first place. The CSU was co-founded in 1889 by Henry Scott Holland, who was then a Canon of St Paul's Cathedral and was to become (in 1910) the Regius Professor of Divinity at Oxford University, and by Charles Gore, who was Principal of Pusey House, also in Oxford. While at Pusey House, Gore founded a religious-monastic community, the Community of the Resurrection. Five of the six founding members of the Society belonged to the CSU. Gore went on to episcopal positions, ultimately as Bishop of Oxford, and was also a highly influential Anglican theologian. Early influences on the CSU were Anglican thinkers such as F. D. Maurice and Charles Kingsley, often termed Christian socialists.

The links with Oxford University were strong. The CSU was established in Oxford. Within a year, it had 77 members. A London branch of the organisation followed and in 1891 this had 124 members. The CSU had three aims. It was to consist of 'members of the Church of England' who agreed: (1) to claim for the Christian law the ultimate authority to rule social practice; (2) to study in common how to apply the moral truths and principles of Christianity to the social and economic problems of the present time; and (3) to present Christ in practical life as the Living Master and King, the enemy of wrong and selfishness, the power of righteousness and love.

There were also links with Cambridge University. The Church of England's Clergy Training School in Cambridge was opened in 1881 and the pioneering New Testament scholar, B. F. Westcott, Regius Professor of Divinity at the University of Cambridge, was the first President. He was also to be the first President of the CSU. At a time when the Church of England was increasingly dominated by two extremes of view, Tractarians and Evangelicals, Westcott was proud to belong to neither. The School's council, constituted in 1887, included the University's divinity professors who were Anglican clergy. In 1899, it moved into permanent buildings in Jesus Lane, Cambridge, and from 1902 it was known as Westcott House.

The academic environment of the early CSU leaders meant that they rarely had direct contact with the social and economic problems of working people. It was not, however, that CSU members deliberately avoided this. The work of the Community of the Resurrection included ministry which reached out to those in need. Scott Holland saw it as part of his work to correspond with leaders of the emerging Labour movement. When Westcott became Chairman of the CSU, he had responsibilities in London as well as Cambridge. His preaching at Westminster Abbey included calls for the Church to be committed to the cause of the disadvantaged. Engagement could take many forms. In 1897, John Carter, the Secretary, stated that, from the CSU's perspective, 'it should always be possible for a sincere Christian to be either a good Tory or a good radical, or even an honest Socialist or a moral Individualist'.

The CSU's primary principles
The CSU considered that one of its main purposes was to bring to the attention of the Church of England its social responsibility. The focus on the Church of England might seem a limitation, but the intention was for the national Church to play a crucial role – to affect the nation. For all its social expression, much of the Union's thinking emerged from a conviction that at the heart of church-life was the Eucharist or Holy Communion, in which the bread and wine were channels of divine grace. Henry Scott Holland linked what he called the 'social solidarity of man' with 'the essential solidarity of Church fellowship', which for him was centred on the body and blood

of Christ received in this sacrament. Indeed, the CSU passed a resolution that its members should have a 'bond of union in the Sacrament of Christ's body'. This was intended to commit them to social service. Scott Holland believed that creating a new social conscience within the life of the Church must involve 'corporate Acts of worship, Communion with one another, in the intimacies of the innermost shrine, gatherings around the one Altar, to partake of the one Bread, and to drink of the one Cup'.

The CSU inclined towards a High Church or Anglo-Catholic position. There was a concern within this stream of thought to uphold in the Church of England the traditions of the 'Church Catholic' – although not Roman Catholic. Emphasis was placed on the role of the priest, with rather less attention being given to the role of lay people. Worship was marked by ceremonies to deepen devotion. However, the CSU included Evangelicals, whose emphases were on conversion, the personal experience of Christ as the one who takes away sin, the Bible as the sole source of authority and an active form of Christian living which was to characterise every believer. Handley Moule, who was a leading Evangelical figure, was a CSU member and was the first Principal of Ridley Hall in Cambridge, a theological college set up to train Evangelicals for Church of England ministry. He was later Bishop of Durham.

Henry Scott Holland spoke of 'the necessity for study' which became another of CSU's key features. It set up small groups to pursue this, in which members would discuss certain books, then try to bring together conclusions they had reached, to be printed and circulated. As well as these local gatherings, there were conferences that drew larger crowds. The main conference each year moved around the country, and was held in cities such as Manchester, Birmingham and Newcastle. While he remained active, Scott Holland was always a major and a persuasive speaker. The impact of all this activity was perceptible. R. H. Tawney, a leading economist, was one of those attracted by this emerging social vision. Tawney's most famous book, *Religion and the Rise of Capitalism*, contained material which he initially presented as the first Henry Scott Holland Memorial Lecture.

The CSU was also optimistic that co-operation was the way to address social issues. Methods seen as confrontational were not encouraged. F. Lewis Donaldson, an Anglican priest who became Archdeacon of Westminster, helped to lead a mass march of the unemployed from Leicester to London in 1905. He believed that this was in line with the concerns of the CSU, of which he was an early member, but it was not regarded favourably by everyone. In the same year, the influential Oxford branch published *Socialism* and, in a rather paternalistic expression of CSU thinking, socialism was described as 'a benevolent movement of the upper classes towards the lower'. In 1906, the CSU's Executive included a Liberal and a Tory MP. Although no one represented the Labour Party, George Lansbury, a future leader of the Party, wrote regularly for CSU's *Commonwealth* magazine. In line with the Labour movement, there was a shared desire to move away from the 'competitive society' to 'co-operative lines'.

New directions

In the years before the First World War, the CSU continued to enjoy considerable support. Membership was around 5,000. Many of the original emphases continued. However, during the war, new directions began to emerge. In 1916, the Archbishops of Canterbury and York launched a National Mission of Repentance and Hope. Within this, they set up a committee (one of five committees convened, covering different topics) to investigate 'the ways in which the Church may best commend the teaching of Christ to those who are seeking to solve the problems of industrial life'. The committee was chaired by E. S. Talbot, Bishop of Winchester, who had long-term involvement in the CSU. The report of the committee, *Christianity and Industrial Problems* (1918), was widely read. Some 25,000 copies were soon printed. A typical point made in the report was: 'We would urge our fellow Christians to ask themselves once more whether an economic system which produces striking inequalities of wealth is compatible with the spirit of Christianity.' Overall, it was significant for the way it advocated varieties of socialist ideas. The reception for this outspoken report was inevitably mixed.

Along with Talbot as chairman, other members of the committee included R. H. Tawney, George Lansbury and Charles Gore, by now Bishop of Oxford. Tawney was particularly active and indeed, in its final form, the *Christianity and Industrial Problems* report was largely his work. Talbot was not convinced about the explicit socialism that was being proposed by some. For his part, Tawney brought to bear on the committee's deliberations his experiences at Toynbee Hall in the East End of London. There he became involved with the Workers' Educational Association (WEA), which had been formed in 1903, and he was an innovative adult education tutor for the WEA as well as – for a short time – a part-time economics lecturer at Glasgow University. In the inter-war years, he was to teach economic history at the London School of Economics. Throughout this whole period, Tawney's Christian socialism, and friendship with William Temple (who was briefly a leader of the CSU and was to emerge as the Church of England's leading figure), would be significant for the Industrial Christian Fellowship as it developed.

To tell a story is more than a matter of describing the landscape that confronts the storyteller, but also to trace within it those particular features and contours that serve the storyteller's purpose. And so, we have to admit that, while these two movements can be depicted as providing the key foundations of an organisation whose time had come, they might also be described as being in terminal decline and ready to clutch at any straw that might secure their future. Churches and missions will often find themselves at such a crossroads, and the key question to be asked is whether they have simply become an end in themselves, in which a few individuals have become so invested that they cannot imagine anything but to continue, or whether their core purpose remains intact – but the new wine of changing circumstances calls for an equivalent new wineskin.

Both can be detected as present within the Navvy Mission as the landscape of Britain shifted in the years immediately following the Great War. Public works were in decline, industrialisation had accelerated, patterns of working had changed and the navvy camp that was the mainstay of its endeavours was simply ceasing to exist. From 1914 onwards, no one became a navvy for the first time, and for those who returned to this life, the transport infrastructure they had built now offered greater mobility, reducing the long-term isolation that had so previously shaped the navvy's identity. Coupled with this were early expressions of what has come to be known as an integrated workforce; life and labour were in a state of flux and required new expressions of Christian presence in the workplace.

In 1919, the NMS changed its name to The Industrial Christian Fellowship (ICF), bringing out what was supposed to be the last edition of the *Quarterly Letter*, the navvy newsletter, shortly afterwards. But within three years it had been re-issued and continued for a further 11 years, albeit with a significantly reduced circulation. For some, it was a matter of remaining a part of the navvy community to the bitter end, for others it was to re-cast its foundational vision in the emerging centres of British industry.

It was evident after the end of the First World War that a new direction for the CSU was equally necessary. The experience and aftermath of the Great War had served to broaden public awareness of many of the issues that it had previously sought to advocate. The challenge was no longer how best to articulate these, but how to put into practice the vision that Talbot's committee had outlined. The newly named Industrial Christian Fellowship had certainly been effective in addressing the needs and challenges it had confronted in the navvy camps, yet could perhaps be justifiably accused of never sufficiently questioning the underlying conditions that caused them.

Lessons in working out our Christian values

The two movements might have seemed very different, but they had influential Anglican backers in common. The CSU brought a vision of a social gospel and the NMS years of experience of reaching working people. By taking 'Fellowship' as part of its name, ICF was also saying that it was something new – neither a Society nor a Union. The three aims of the CSU were incorporated into the aims of the new Fellowship along with all the tradition and practice that was contained within NMS. As well as the study aspect, the Fellowship committed itself to reaching out spiritually and socially to all in the industrial world, which would mean reaching far beyond navvies. ICF brought together a desire that people working in industry would be brought to faith in Christ, with a vision to unite all classes in a bond of Christian fellowship.

Yet there is always a danger that well-intentioned interventions by those in positions of power and advantage can nonetheless reinforce the injustices and divisions they seek to address. In his book *Christian Socialism: Scott Holland to Tony Blair* (London, SCM, 1998), Alan Wilkinson gives a picture of its development and the culture within which it evolved. He highlights those of great Christian and social conscience, but his account stands as a warning for a middle-class church seeking to address the problems of the poor. In the course of discussing William Morris, for example, Wilkinson recounts the experience of a former kitchen-maid who recalled how she slaved below stairs late at night and early in the morning to serve Morris and his friends upstairs who were discussing socialism.

The author also similarly observes an incident in the wake of William Temple's formation of the Life and Liberty group during the First World War. He recounts that Oswin Creighton, son of a former Bishop of London, was one of those perceptive Great War chaplains who – like Studdert Kennedy – were agonised by the gulf between the Church and the experience of those on the battlefields. In 1918, shortly before he was killed, he described how he had spent the afternoon and evening in drenching rain, helping to load up ambulances with the wounded and the dying. 'Then I got a memorandum from Life and Liberty asking what the men are thinking about the self-government of the Church' (a proposal with which

Temple was engaged). There were exceptions – the slum priests and those who dedicated their lives to working among the disadvantaged of society. NMS very much belonged in this group, bringing this dimension to the newly formed organisation in a world where much social and Christian concern was distanced from those for whom care was expressed.

An exploration of the nineteenth-century background described above is helped through a consideration of the life of William Lovett, the Chartist; Robert Owen's communal gospel; Matthew Arnold's social unity; and John Ruskin's view of work and society. Yet it is clear that the French Revolution and its atheistic results provoked a fear that held back the social reformers. However, following the Irish potato famine of the 1840s, John Bright did attack the Government for keeping the wages of labourers down, and Charles Kingsley told the Chartists in 1848: 'We have used the Bible as if it were the special constable's handbook – an opium dose for keeping beasts of burden patient while they were being overloaded – a mere book to keep the poor in order.'

A. S. Peake (the biblical scholar), after reading William Booth's *In Darkest England, and the Way Out*, wrote:

> The poor are Christ's representatives. He has identified himself everywhere with the down-trodden, the suffering and the outcast. Inasmuch as we do good to one of these we do it to him. We serve God by helping our fellow. I feel intensely that privilege implies responsibility.

These views are echoed in the thinking of the Christian Social Union. To a twenty-first-century reader, such perspectives might appear somewhat mainstream to Christian political thinking, but at the time this was far from the case, and ICF was seeking to gather and develop a stream of thought that, in its day, was both radical and necessary.

We are challenged by Charles Gore's words to a Bournemouth priest who complained that nothing stopped his conventional congregation from attending church: 'Have you ever tried preaching the Gospel?' Gore saw the Labour movement summed up as: *Not charity but justice*. The wealth of the nation did not lie in commodities but in people living healthy, happy lives; and Temple learned from Reinhold Niebuhr that 'love' in social organisation is 'justice', but he remained optimistic of a top-down social policy.

There are lessons for us to learn from these early years of Christian engagement with work and workers. Christian thinking about social justice and the value of every human life has to be lived out in the action of the Church and its members.

The next chapter looks at how these issues were worked out in the early years of the newly formed organisation.

Chapter 2

The early development of the Fellowship

A launderer's field just outside Jerusalem and the cloisters of an ancient royal palace may not seem the most natural places to begin the next chapter in The Industrial Christian Fellowship's (ICF's) story, but this is a movement that has often been described as 'prophetic', so we might reasonably expect that the lives and actions of the prophets of the Old Testament would offer a perspective on its history. The locations in question appear in the seventh chapters of the books of Isaiah and Amos respectively. Each represents a confrontation between the biblical prophet and the authorities of their day: Isaiah and the king; Amos and the official court prophet Amaziah. Both are set at a time in the nation's history when the future is uncertain, military threat is looming and key decisions about the future direction need to be taken.

Although the national scene into which the Fellowship was launched could at least put the First World War behind it, what was far less clear was how the nation might now recover and progress during peace. The conflict had brought to a head a number of realities, many of which were already gathering pace in the years before it. The introduction of women's suffrage for example, while significant in its own right, is also representative of a wider movement where those who were excluded and disenfranchised were increasingly refusing to accept the narrative that this was 'their lot' and were looking for a fairer and redefined structure for society.

The war had not only been won in the trenches. Just as the carnage had been on an industrial scale, so its triumph was also one of industrial manufacturing, logistics and supply chains in which the munitions and armaments factories along with other manufacturers had played a crucial part. At one level therefore, the Allied victory revealed the incredible potential that could be achieved when industrialists, politicians and of course ordinary people could be brought together in common accord, yet it also revealed the damage that this could inflict if its purpose was misplaced.

The king who met the prophet in the laundry fields of Jerusalem was faced with the kind of international threat that ministers and politicians imagined, at the time, the Great War had put behind them. But like that ancient monarch, they needed to consider where to place their trust if they were to build a new and prosperous world for their citizens. It was clear that they needed the support and favour of appropriate allies and needed to discern, from a growing mass of conflicting voices, who those allies should be.

All of this lay before the leading lights of the newly formed Industrial Christian Fellowship as they sought to bring together the ideas and experience of the two organisations from which it had been crafted. It was clear not only that the social and economic structures that prevailed in the years before war would not emerge unscathed, but also the Church was recognised as being part of those discredited structures. Yet before them also was a vision of what could be achieved if that spirit of common endeavour, that had been deployed to such deadly effect in a period of conflict, could be harnessed for good in pursuit of the Kingdom of God.

As the Old Testament prophets bear witness, this would depend upon being able to offer a convincing and compelling vision of divine purpose to those who held power. Yet this also generated internal challenges for the community of faith. The dispute between Amaziah and Amos was not simply between the king and the prophet, but over who could truly represent God's message. It is easy to depict Amaziah and Amos simply as irreconcilable opponents, and the separation of centuries makes it impossible to know the precise details of their confrontation. But a genuine tension emerges from the narrative: to what degree should prophets secure their place within the structures of power, perhaps at times tempering their message to ensure that they retain the ear of those with influence, and to what degree should they remain uncompromisingly true to their convictions, even if this means their message falling on deaf ears. Though the early members of ICF might not have so openly recognised this tension, it can be detected in many of their early debates and meetings.

Note has already been made of the newly formed Fellowship's pre-history and how the Navvy Mission Society (NMS) brought a proven ability to engage and influence an element in society that was otherwise largely excluded and disaffected. Something else that might be detected in those early beginnings was the move to bring varied and disparate efforts into a single entity with national scope. This not only created an economy of scale for the organisation itself, but enabled it to be a recognisable element within navvy life and culture. The navvies' *Quarterly Letter* had included such things as lists of vacancies in new projects, so while unstinting in its purpose to promote Christian faith, it also served as something equivalent to a trade journal. Comments, like those from the Mayor of Ludlow, recorded in the previous chapter, highlight the very real impact that such a movement might have on civic life more generally. In the early decades after the war, religious and political leaders alike were increasingly recognising that 'those in power' included ordinary people who – through guilds, trade unions and general social trends – were becoming a voice of growing significance in their own right. From 1920, that legacy was coupled and significantly impacted by the powerful influence and academic rigour of the Christian Social Union. A movement that could genuinely converge these two streams had real potential to play a significant role in emerging society.

The person who more than anyone else was responsible for this union and its subsequent development was Paul Thomas Radford-Rowe Kirk, usually known as P. T. R. Kirk. He studied at Trinity College, Dublin, and then had Anglican curacies in Ireland and England, before becoming Vicar of St Mary Magdalene, Peckham. He was a Chaplain to the Armed Forces during the First World War and then became the first General Director of ICF. He was so single-minded that he rarely took a holiday. This chapter looks at the way in which the movement developed under Kirk's leadership in the 1920s. During this period, it was seen to a large extent within Anglican circles as a 'home missionary society' of the Church of England, and its office in London was connected with Church House. Kirk's vision for the Fellowship – as we will see – was a broader one.

Developing the aims of ICF
As with the Christian Social Union (CSU), the Industrial Christian Fellowship had three main aims, and much of the wording that CSU used in its definitive statements was retained. With ICF, however, there was a stress on seeking to win those in industrial life 'to personal discipleship of Jesus Christ, and to unite all classes in a bond of Christian fellowship and prayer'. Also, study was to be undertaken explicitly 'under the guidance of the Holy Spirit'. More was said about these aims as time went on. Minute

books of the early 1920s record discussions at which it was agreed that a major purpose was 'to unite for intercession and service those within the Christian Church who believe it is a part of the Church's province to make justice and love the controlling motives in all change'. In addition, ICF was 'prepared to support all movements towards a new and better order which have for their fundamental object the recognition of Christ and his teaching'. This was evidence that those who formed ICF wanted not only to reach those in industry, as the NMS had done for navvies, but anticipated a transformative impact on society more generally. Rather than being a 'home missionary society' on the Church of England's behalf, they saw themselves as shaping its thinking and actions, and those of movements beyond it. Later, ICF affirmed the aim of 'federating the work of all societies which have for their object a more Christian Social Order'.

One of the other movements with a vision for a better social order was the Church Socialist League (CSL), which had been founded in 1906 and was promoted by – among others – Lewis Donaldson. It carried on some of the ideals of the earlier Guild of St Matthew, which came to an end in 1909. There was overlap between ICF and the CSL; George Lansbury and R. H. Tawney were among those involved in both. In February 1922, an informal conference was convened between representatives from ICF and from the CSL. Although the CSL included Free Church leaders – John Clifford, a towering Baptist figure, had been a chairman – this meeting had an Anglican flavour. P. T. R. Kirk and Tawney took an active part in exploring possibilities for future co-operation. However, the CSL was already struggling to maintain its socialist identity and it came to an end in 1923. Possible ICF co-operation with the short-lived Christian Social Crusade (1920–1926) was also investigated. Despite these efforts, the aim of wider joint action through 'federation' was fulfilled only in limited ways.

Under Kirk's leadership, ICF had its own agenda. In the aftermath of the First World War, it wanted to bring a challenge in various areas. On the one hand, it spoke against those who saw Christianity as merely 'dope' administered to the 'unfortunate' by the 'fortunate' to keep them quiet and in their place. Religion, ICF noted, was also often discussed – when it was discussed at all – in 'a casual or condescending way'. At the same time, the Fellowship aimed to challenge the Church of England to look critically at the traditional way in which its parishes operated. Kirk was convinced that in general they were ill-equipped to address the spiritual and social needs of industrial workers. Some of the issues raised by ICF included what was termed the 'fight between the machine and man', especially the need for men and women in industrial life to 'count as persons'; the importance of 'living wage conditions'; and actions to improve 'safety' at work. It also initiated discussions of 'workers' rights and the responsibilities of employers. A proposal within ICF that the Fellowship should advocate workers having a say in the running of the enterprise where they were employed was regarded favourably by some, but did not gain enough approval for it to be accepted as formal policy. Discussions of this kind would continue to be a feature of the Fellowship's life. The fact that a newly formed Christian organisation could be defined by introducing to the public arena issues that would largely be taken for granted today, explains something of why it was perceived as necessary and perhaps also why, with time, it struggled to sustain its own distinct identity.

There is no doubt that Kirk's vision, tenacity and influential connections enabled ICF to develop an effective and well-organised infrastructure and, in this aspect of its mission, it proved itself to be a significant success. But the Fellowship saw itself as existing for more than that, and to understand its vision fully, we need to focus further on the social and political realities of life in Britain after the First World War. What had caused thousands of men to enlist and entailed the sacrifice of fathers, husbands and sons from every strata of society, was a belief that the cause for which they were fighting was worthwhile. But the experience of the trenches not only exposed the immense human cost of that, but also began to break down some of the traditional barriers in society and expose the flaws in the national identity they were seeking to defend. As already highlighted, this was not so much a realisation that suddenly dawned, but the acceleration of a stream of consciousness that had already been gathering momentum in the preceding years.

More and more the narrative became one that was not so much about defending the way of life they had inherited, but more about fighting for the freedom to build a new order; one that would reward the endeavours of those who had sacrificed so much. But this raised some crucial questions. What would be the building blocks of this new order? What values would define it? What sense of shared identity would bring people together in pursuit of its realisation? No longer could the working masses, retained in the grip of poverty, be expected to provide the labour to generate the wealth of the privileged few. They needed new incentives to be engaged in this new society and this needed to be gained by a new sense of common purpose and mutual interaction.

The war period had shown the effectiveness of politicians and industrialists working together to maintain effective and highly productive supply chains. The future potential of such partnerships was obvious, but in whose interests should these now be formed? Should industry exist solely to reward and generate profit for its investors and directors? To what degree should it serve some defined national interest? And to what degree should it now be influenced and operated to more justly reward the endeavours of the labourers and tradespeople without whom it would simply not function? While these questions to some degree remain, they were far more fluid and contested in the period in which ICF was formed.

Another key feature of the landscape was a sense of betrayal. The Great Depression caused devastating unemployment in many industrial centres, so for many people, once again thrown into appalling poverty, the question was not so much how this new order should be formed, but why it had failed to materialise at all.

It is against this backdrop that the title 'Industrial Christian Fellowship' reveals its significance. One undisputed fact was that this needed to be a period of industrial expansion, yet for those who made up the councils and committees of ICF, there was a belief that if this new order was to avoid the divisions and injustices of times past, Christian values needed to be at its heart. Their vision today might be taken for granted, but at the time Christianity for too many was expressed primarily through involvement in their Christian communities, not by embedding the teachings of Christ into industrial and commercial practice. And if the various strands of society were to be brought together in pursuit of this new vision, as the old class strata began to erode, a new sense of cohesion would be achieved through the principle of 'fellowship' – identifying and articulating the common cause in which the conflicting aspirations could be harnessed. For its most ambitious proponents, 'Industrial Christian Fellowship' might justifiably be described not as their vision for an institution, but for the nation as a whole. And the growing sense of betrayal gave an added urgency to their task.

While there is no doubt that at the heart of Kirk's endeavours was the establishment and maintenance of an effective organisation, many of the influential figures who enlisted in its ranks did not so much see the organisation as an end in itself, but were genuinely committed to a forum where the bonds of co-operation and identity could be formed. One such example would be Lionel Hitchens, the Chairman of the Cammell Laird shipyard in Birkenhead, Merseyside, and one of ICF's trustees for well over a decade. Hitchens had been a close associate of Viscount Milner while he was High Commissioner for South Africa. Milner had returned to Britain to become a key member of Lloyd George's War Cabinet and was a significant figure in the structuring of post-war society. Hitchens too had played an influential role, heading up a diplomatic mission on behalf of Lloyd George to set up what became the Imperial Munitions Board. Although Britain's colonial influence was beginning to wane, Hitchens represented a generation who were well used to the close association of industry and politics in the arena of international development. He was a highly competent individual who had played a key role in establishing and organising 'collective action' – the coming together of key industries in a unified war effort. This left him with a vision and enthusiasm for the potential of rationalised and integrated industrial expansion where the conflicting interests highlighted above could come together in common cause. He would be one of many who saw a shared sense of Christian identity as the key strand in achieving this. The presence of individuals like him explains why ICF was able to exert such influence at the time, yet it might reasonably be questioned whether his key concern was the organisation itself or the ends that its endeavours could be harnessed to achieve.

This principle of 'fellowship' was first tested, with limited success, when representatives of ICF sought to become involved in the coal industry crisis of 1921. There was a trade depression and coal exports from Britain slumped. The Government returned the coal mines to private ownership and the owners promptly demanded wage cuts. Strike action by miners resulted. Kirk and Henry Carter, a well-known Methodist minister, attempted to draw together leaders from across the denominations to play a role in this time of crisis. ICF considered that there was a right to strike and that conciliation and arbitration were crucial for constructive industrial relations. At the time, a united front from the churches was not achieved to the extent that Kirk had hoped. In 1926, with further and more far-reaching strike action by miners, Kirk convened an *ad hoc* committee to try to find a compromise. This ultimately proved a failure, despite Kirk's best efforts.

This perhaps revealed something of the scale of the task that lay ahead. If there was to be a successful defining of industrial endeavour around the principles of Christian fellowship then a serious process of engagement and learning needed to be undertaken. The Church needed to recognise the urgency of engaging in the life of industrial communities and to acknowledge the prevailing injustices in urban centres. Industrialists and politicians needed to be held to account against the values of Christian faith and practice, and ordinary people needed to be convinced of a Christian identity that would hold them fast to the collective vision that emerged. As we trace ICF's early endeavours, it cannot be denied that it engaged earnestly in its task, seeking to weave a sense of Christian identity into every aspect of industrial society.

Allegiance to Christ

While Kirk espoused this comprehensive vision for ICF, he genuinely wanted to see individuals in the workplace coming to allegiance to Christ through the witness of committed followers of Jesus. For him those aspects not only belonged together, but his desire to see working people re-engaged with the narrative of Christian faith was of immeasurable value in its own right. The Navvy Mission Society had concentrated on reaching individuals, although along with the presentation of the Christian message, significant social care had always been seen as integral to that. It was a core achievement of Kirk's to see this fusion of evangelism and the wider application of Christian faith to social life embodied in ICF. Some of the NMS missionaries continued in their role, but since ICF wanted to reach out much more broadly to workers in industry, new missionaries began to be recruited. Because the missioners (as they were now generally called) had to travel around visiting different sites, a number of unmarried men were initially appointed.

Kirk took a direct personal interest in this, to the extent that some would describe him as controlling. This is reflected in the records of the recruitment process. In 1920, the members of ICF's interviewing committee were impressed by a single man aged twenty-six, by another unmarried man who was aged thirty-one, and by someone aged thirty-four who was described as 'a Christian Socialist'. A number of applicants had experience of open-air meetings. The 'Christian Socialist' had been a speaker in Hyde Park in London and it was noted that he was aware of social and industrial problems. Those applicants who were over forty were often turned down. One application which definitely did not fit was from someone aged sixty-seven, who was an ex-serviceman. There were also doubts about those who did not wish to spend time away from their families. Most of those appointed were in their twenties and thirties and those who had worked in industry and had practical experience of leading services and/or speaking in the open air were especially favoured. A number were already trained lay readers in the Church of England and all received thorough training from ICF. All applicants had to supply a reference from their vicars and in one case, with someone who was not Anglican, it was stipulated that he needed to be confirmed. The annual salary for the missioners was £350 (the rough equivalent of £15,000 today), plus travelling expenses.

In 1924, ICF began to recruit women to reach out to workplaces where women were employed. As with the men, the preferred age group was in the twenties and thirties. Although the hope was that women who had experience of industrial work could be appointed, applicants with this kind of background were relatively rare. It was more typical for younger teachers to be employed, as they had leadership experience. One of those appointed was recognised as having had involvement with young people from a range of backgrounds through expeditions with Scouts and Guides. Another regarded as suitable had been a history teacher, had connections with adult education in Cambridge, but had also been a welfare worker. Many of the applicants were considered unsuitable, usually on account of their age. ICF took an interest in the work of what had been the Women's Trade Union League, which in 1921, under the leadership of the influential Mary Macarthur, became the Women's Section of the Trades Union Congress. What becomes clear is that the Fellowship was able to attract a diverse group of individuals, and was clearly reflecting its commitment to draw together a broad range of interests into a common Christian fellowship.

The band of missioners grew to 40 men and women. This was the peak. As well as visiting places of work – such as factories, docks and mines – and speaking to individuals, outreach meetings were held in halls, clubs and in the open air. Visits were also made to families where a family member was in hospital or in prison. Often a special mission – or 'crusade' as they were commonly called – would be held in a particular area, usually in larger centres of population. These crusades, first initiated at Woolwich in 1919 by William Hough, who had recently been appointed Bishop of Woolwich, were organised by the Fellowship in collaboration with local Church of England clergy. Typically, they brought together a large team, and the events included a number of meetings, several in the open air, conducted over about a fortnight. Hough described the crusade as an effort to break down barriers. He hoped it would induce those who were outside Church organisations, but not necessarily antagonistic to religion, to hear the way in which Christianity might bring light to bear on the complex problems of the day. ICF, similarly, spoke of the way missions could remove prejudices, and could make those who heard talks willing to learn more. As the pattern of crusades developed, extensive mission preparation took place, in some cases for two years before the event itself. Cities and towns considered strategic for missioners and mission outreach included London,

Glasgow, Manchester, Sheffield, Darlington, Middlesbrough, Birmingham, Nottingham, Bristol, Swansea and Southampton.

Industrial initiatives

ICF also undertook a number of initiatives related to industry which had a wider impact. One of these was the designation of one Sunday in the year – the Sunday before May Day – as 'Industrial Sunday'. It was felt by Kirk that the religious observance on that day would influence the tone and character of the May Day celebrations. He persuaded some Labour leaders in 1920 to support a letter to trade union secretaries commending the new idea of Industrial Sunday as a time to 'commit their movement to God, and seek afresh a share of His vision and ideals'. Support was forthcoming, and by 1923 Industrial Sunday had become a feature of many Anglican and Free Church congregations. Kirk broadcast a radio message each year, starting in 1921. He encouraged prayers and preaching on that Sunday to take up themes relevant to Christian faith in relation to industry. It was more difficult for churches following the lectionary to adapt the sermons to take in this aspect, but there was an impact. One press report in 1924 spoke of hundreds of churches to which working people, in groups according to their trade unions, and in many cases with their employers, marched on Industrial Sunday. ICF took some satisfaction from the evident 'co-operation of all engaged in industry', and hoped that it would bring closer 'what we may call, without reserve, the Kingdom of God on earth'. For ICF this had broad appeal, not only to committed Christians: 'Unselfishness rather than self-interest, and the better service of mankind as the goal of industry, are surely the spiritual aims in which all men of goodwill can unite.'

The impact of ICF on wider Christian thinking about the Church and industrial society was also seen in COPEC, the Conference on Christian Politics, Economics and Citizenship, which attracted 1,500 leaders in church and society (80 from outside Britain) to Birmingham for a week in 1924. It was chaired by William Temple, who was then Bishop of Manchester and who would come to have great significance in the ICF story. Preparation for COPEC had gone on for four years. P. T. R. Kirk and J. A. Kempthorne, who was Bishop of Lichfield and Chairman of ICF, were among those who prepared the material for the event, and both were on its Executive Committee. As a result of the study that was undertaken in various COPEC 'commissions' in 1924, a range of volumes was produced, including one on 'Christianity and Industry' and one on 'The Social Function of the Church'.

Both contained outspoken statements about how industry was requiring 'the motive of gain' to replace 'the motive of service'. Under the heading 'Industry and Property' it was alleged, in forthright terms, that the present industrial system was 'not merely defective, but vicious and radically unchristian'.

It is doubtful that all those involved would have gone as far as that, but such sentiments did draw attention to ICF as a Christian voice to be noted in the industrial world. In April 1926, an article in *The Spectator* gave positive attention to these endeavours. The Fellowship, it stated, stood for 'the doctrine that Christianity should concern itself with the conditions of industrial life', which seemed 'admirable'. However, the article accepted that there were disturbing stories circulating of some ICF meetings being indistinguishable from socialist meetings. These allegations provoked occasional denunciations. One of these appeared in 1926 in the *Morning Post*, a newspaper (later taken over by the *Daily Telegraph*) which advocated conservative social and political perspectives. For its editor, the 'frequent interventions into politics' made by ICF were always 'on the Socialist side' and in its approach to industrial society in Britain the Fellowship was branded as 'an agent of the Labour Party'. It was claimed, without evidence, that ICF had favoured the Bolsheviks in Russia and had even justified their secularisation of the Christian Sunday.

The constant accusations of socialism and the emerging presence of the Labour Party highlight the tensions that were outlined in the introduction to this chapter. ICF worked hard to maintain a non-partisan approach and to identify itself as espousing a genuinely Christian vision. While some remained committed to that difficult but potentially more beneficial arena of bringing various parties together to discern a shared Christian narrative, many people of faith found it easier to align themselves with the emerging political movements of the day.

The reality was that, in the 1920s, the main channel through which ICF operated and sought to have its initiatives affirmed was not the Labour Party nor any other socialist movement but the Church of England. The Presidents of ICF in this period were the Archbishops of Canterbury and York. Its Vice-President and Chairman were Anglican bishops, and there was always a large contingent of bishops on its Council. The lay members of the Council in the later 1920s alongside Lionel Hitchens included Major-General Sir Frederick Maurice and Lady Maurice; Lord Henry Bentinck; Vice-Admiral Sydney Drury-Lowe; Miss Constance Smith, OBE; Miss Irene Cox, OBE; the Hon. Gertrude M. Kinnaird; Lady Angela Malcolm;

and Sir Benjamin Sands Johnson and Sir Robert Lowden Connell, both from Liverpool and perhaps linked with Hitchens. Of the relatively few trade union leaders who were active supporters of ICF, H. H. Elvin, President of the Trades Union Congress, Frank Hodges, Secretary of the Miners' Federation, and Fred Hughes of the National Union of Clerks were prominent. A small number of Labour MPs were involved: examples were Charles G. Ammon, who was also Secretary of the Union of Post Office Workers, Somerville Hastings, the son of a Congregational minister, and Morgan Jones, who was the first conscientious objector to be elected to Parliament after the First World War. Out of what was then a very large ICF Executive of 40 members (it became much smaller later), only three could be classed as 'Labour men'.

This might reflect something of the dilemma that ICF faced. Its genuine commitment to a broad, non-partisan fellowship is evident from its participants and its structures, yet its attempts to speak into the public square often resulted from it being associated with the partisan group whose narrative most closely resembled its own. ICF had a widely read monthly publication, *The Torch*, and each copy made it clear that it was 'not a political but a spiritual movement'. The topics covered included hours of work; the intellectual and physical deterioration of the large numbers of unemployed, especially during the depression of the later 1920s; Christianity and the race question; housing, and materials used in the building trade; concern for those who would now be described as having learning disabilities; the problems of tied cottages when workers lost their jobs; health provision for all; and support for families and family allowances. In all these areas, there were calls for initiatives that would promote improvements for working people. In some articles there were tentative explorations of potential commonalities between Christianity and communism (although not atheistic communism), but there were also articles by, for example, Lord Eustace Percy, a Conservative politician and diplomat. The Fellowship certainly saw some aspects of its role as implying a spiritual revolution, but never an enforced socialist regime. William Temple, concerned to clarify matters, wrote in defence of ICF, and his defence carried weight. This was part of ICF's vision, to educate and inform in pursuit of a genuine belief that – rather than forming around conflicting interests – it was possible to create an industrial landscape where these could be brought together in pursuit of a higher Christian purpose.

Education and training

Education was a particular area of concern for ICF. A number of its publications argued that there should be generous expenditure on education for the rising generation, that the school leaving age – the age of compulsory education for all – should be raised to fifteen, and that there should be an increase in secondary school accommodation. It also highlighted the need for more places in special schools for pupils needing particular help. In the 1920s, special classrooms began to be created within schools for pupils who could not keep up with the learning pace in general education. ICF was not speaking about these issues from a theoretical standpoint: staff members and other representatives visited schools, youth organisations, colleges and universities. Organisations that offered education to adults also received the backing of the Fellowship. Such adult education had been a feature of the Navvy Mission Society and what they also had in common was an established commitment not simply to see this as a channel through which to articulate its own beliefs, but also through which it could learn from those it encountered so as to articulate their concerns in the public arena. There were also links with the Workers' Educational Association (WEA) and, through R. H. Toynbee and William Temple, who was a President of the WEA, there was a CSU strand in this relationship.

Another aspect of ICF's commitment to education was its work within Anglican parishes. In addition to publishing *The Torch* and a range of pamphlets, the Fellowship produced several study guides which could be used by groups – often called study circles – that wanted to look at the social dimensions of the Christian faith. The motto for the educational aspect was 'Christ, the Lord of all Life'. A book with that title was published and went through many editions. ICF set up its own Study Department and had a book-room and a well-stocked library – again reminiscent of the Navvy Mission Society. Meetings of smaller ICF groups led to larger-scale conferences. Increasingly, through the 1920s, the Fellowship was able to promote research into Christian approaches to contemporary problems. Conferences and workshops drew together clergy, industrialists and economists. The work that followed on from COPEC, in which Kirk was deeply involved, provided opportunities for a partnership that extended beyond Anglicanism to take in the Free Churches, something which Kirk saw as of great importance. There was a group that drew together research carried out by COPEC and ICF, and also a research group led by Tom Pym, Anglican Dean of Camberwell, who was Head of Cambridge House, which had links with Cambridge University and published the *Cambridge House Bulletin*, which addressed industrial issues.

Education and training were seen by ICF as crucial for its missioners. Here the main responsibility lay with William G. Peck, a Methodist minister who became an Anglican in 1925. In that year he published his book, *The Divine Society: Christian Dogma and Social Redemption* (London: SCM), which was widely regarded as representing a milestone in Anglican social thought. Peck, who had embraced the Anglo-Catholic tradition, argued that the hope that was being placed in modern secular constructions of society was proving unfounded. It was within Christianity that a sound basis for social structure was to be discovered – or rediscovered. Peck was not afraid to speak of 'the political implications of the Christian Faith'. He recognised a deep-seated divergence between the Christian outlook and the secular one: for him 'Christian dogma must be set in opposition to those secular assumptions which now govern human relations'. Pursuing a theme that would often be taken up, Peck placed 'fellowship' above the 'false individualism' of the time in which he was writing. Fellowship was rooted in Christian belief in the Holy Trinity. Peck argued that:

> the Christian Faith reinforces this consideration [about fellowship] with the most profound and daring sanction, declaring that even within the Being of God personality exists only in social relation. The doctrine of the Holy Trinity is far from being a purely academic construction without meaning for practical affairs. It lies at the root of the Christian ethic. It signifies that God is both personal and social, both completely, both at once: that within His infinite Being the relation of love is for ever maintained.

The theologically demanding training required of missioners normally took place over two years and included what was also required of Anglican lay readers. However, the ICF courses added a number of other topics, such as social and economic history, social psychology, and the origins and development of industrial organisation, with special reference to the trade union movement. The work of Christian social reformers was discussed: William Wilberforce and other members of the 'Clapham Sect'; George Stringer Bull, who was active in the 1830s in seeking improvement in working conditions; and the Evangelical Lord Shaftesbury, who was notable for his involvement in wide-ranging issues of social reform. The work of those who had been addressing the challenges of the twentieth century was also discussed. Among these was Basil Jellicoe, a Church of

England clergyman who studied at Oxford and became founder of the St Pancras Housing Association and several other housing associations in London, Sussex and Cornwall. Another twentieth-century figure was Charles Jenkinson, who studied at Cambridge and also became a housing reformer. In 1927, Jenkinson requested appointment to 'the hardest parish in the country' and was assigned one of the worst slums in Leeds. By the end of the 1920s, models of ministry for ICF were well established.

Fostering fellowship

As has already been outlined, alongside the crucially important engagement in industrial mission and Christian theology were determined efforts to create a sense of the reality of fellowship. The London office was named Fellowship House. For a small amount per annum – affordable for those it was seeking to reach – it was possible to be a subscriber to ICF and to receive *The Torch*. This was a way of bonding together those involved and modelling a principle that was core to its vision. In 1928/29, the number of subscribers was about 12,000. This was to prove a high point. One of the missioners claimed in that year that each week more than 1,500 workers heard the Christian message brought by someone from the Fellowship, not including sermons given to church congregations and meetings held in the open air. By 1934/35, the number of subscribers had dropped to 9,000. From then on there were attempts to promote fellowship in new ways, such as through the creation of small cells. Although subscriptions brought in income, the ongoing work was also dependent on donations from those able to offer greater financial support. Despite much goodwill, finance was an ongoing issue.

It was P. T. R. Kirk, above anyone else, who brought people together. He was always on the look-out to make new connections. He was particularly gifted at recognising the distinctive contribution that individuals could make to ICF's work. He was also alive to new ideas that came from different sources. In 1925, he led a delegation which included 15 ICF members to a 'Life and Work' World Conference (a precursor to the World Council of Churches) in Stockholm. There were, however, some tensions created because of the varied people Kirk sought to include. His own inclusive vision, going beyond the Church of England to embrace the Free Churches, was not – at least at first – that espoused by William Peck, who in 1928 stated that the contribution of the Church of England must be made 'upon the Catholic basis'. Peck saw any attempt to treat the English Church as one of a number of Protestant communions as a 'ludicrous' exercise. In his view, the Free Churches were deficient in their sacramental theology. What enabled Kirk's broader understanding of fellowship to prevail was that there was a shared commitment among all those associated with ICF to a social vision. Peck expressed this in his own way, proposing that a slum tenement was 'as derogatory to the Holy Ghost' as would be 'a Mass celebrated with mouldy bread and a dirty chalice'. Evangelicals would have used different words, but the desire for change was a common theme.

In the 1920s, ICF was pleased to receive the backing of a range of bishops in the Church of England, both Anglo-Catholic and Evangelical. It also deployed Anglican resources in various ways. For example, Area Directors were appointed to oversee the work of the missioners and these were typically related to a group of five or six Anglican dioceses. Most of the Directors – typically there were six at any one time – were ordained Anglican clergymen. They travelled around speaking to groups and preaching. A small headquarters staff in London co-ordinated activities nationally.

Yet for all its commitment to fellowship, a serious deficiency was that the workers who were being reached were hardly ever represented on the Executive or the wider Council of ICF. Most meetings of these bodies were held on weekday mornings or afternoons, which those in factory-type work could not attend. Nonetheless, at the grassroots there was a sense of belonging. Charles Raven, who was one of the two central organisers of COPEC, and who was regarded as the most effective preacher within the Church of England in this period, saw in ICF an example of the kind of fellowship for which he hoped. He called for commitment to 'community, the *koinonia* of the Holy Spirit'. This *koinonia*, coming out of COPEC, led in 1929 to the formation of a national Council of Christian Churches for Social Questions, more commonly known as the Christian Social Council, with the Fellowship playing a creative part in what was an interdenominational agency for Christian social involvement.

There is more yet to be said about this period in ICF's history, but it already becomes evident that it was more successful at articulating its message within the confines of Christianity than in wider society. Many who espoused its ideals, and remained faithful in their support, nonetheless pursued more influential and less complicated channels through which to achieve their ambitions. The tension represented by Amos and Amaziah remains present in Christian social action to this day. To what degree should it remain true to its core identity even at the expense of achieving its objectives, and to what degree should it allow itself to be shaped by the opportunities and pragmatic realities of the field in which it seeks to operate, for the sake of achieving its noble ends? There is no doubt that ICF remained wedded to its Christian ideals, though many of the social changes attributed to political and trade union-initiated reforms were undertaken by individuals with no less an association to the Fellowship. But before this is explored further, there is one particularly remarkable figure whose story needs to be told. This is examined in the next chapter.

Chapter 3

Geoffrey Studdert Kennedy: ICF's 'Special Messenger'

The words of Proverbs 29 often find their way into our contemporary life – 'Where there is no vision, the people perish' – but it is perhaps also true that where there are not those with the energy and capacity to take it forward, the vision perishes. Geoffrey Anketell Studdert Kennedy (1883–1929) was the best-known ICF figure in the 1920s and might well be described as one such person. The previous chapter highlights the visionary role that P. T. R. Kirk played in the formation of the movement, but also notes his effectiveness in what we more recently might describe as 'networking'. Studdert Kennedy was one of those people that Kirk recognised as being potentially vital to ICF's grassroots impact and he arranged for him to become ICF's 'Special Messenger'. In so doing, he created a synergy that would last well beyond Studdert Kennedy's tragically short lifetime.

Studdert Kennedy was a unique and unconventional figure, his idiosyncrasies exaggerated by life circumstances that also became the cradle for ICF's vision to accelerate forwards in the years after the First World War. It is impossible to know how the movement would have fared without the impetus and attention that he brought to its work, or indeed whether Studdert Kennedy would have generated the reputation that he did, without the raft of opportunities that ICF created, although there is evidence to suggest that much of that reputation was already well established before he was appointed their Messenger. The simple truth is that they came together at a crucial moment, not only in their own histories, but in the history of a nation that was bruised and uncertain, with its leaders and ordinary citizens alike yearning for change.

Studdert Kennedy's parents were born in Ireland but he was brought up in a very poor area of Leeds, where his father was Vicar of St Mary's, Quarry Hill. After secondary education at Leeds Grammar School, Geoffrey became a student at Trinity College, Dublin, where in 1904 he graduated, with distinction, in classics and divinity. From Dublin he took a post as a teacher at Calday Grange Grammar School on the Wirral peninsula. With his love of teaching, learning and laughter, he enjoyed this environment. During this period, he felt called to Anglican ministry and left to train at the former Yorkshire Ripon Clergy College, which had moved to Birmingham in 1902, later to move to Oxford in 1919 and finally to merge with Cuddesdon College as Ripon College Cuddesdon in 1975. His curacies were at Rugby Parish Church, where he developed work in a slum area, and then alongside his father in Leeds. He married Emily Catlow in 1914 and later that year became Vicar of St Paul's, Worcester. When the First World War broke out, he applied for a commission as a chaplain and it was during the war that he gained a national reputation as a spell-binding preacher. This chapter looks briefly at Studdert Kennedy's ministry prior to his years with ICF, but concentrates on his years with the Fellowship.

A journey in ministry

History has largely defined Studdert Kennedy through his role as a First World War chaplain, and it is certainly true that his captivating addresses to the troops, rooted in a theology that refused to gloss over the realities and horrors of the trenches, earned him a deserved reputation. But his role with ICF, coupled with parish ministry, might also be described as allowing him to pursue a purpose that was already evident before the war began.

It was while still a curate that he was recognised as a gifted speaker, including preaching in the open air. In Worcester, he attempted to reach out to all those in the St Paul's parish, through visiting local pubs, holding open-air services and debates, and finding out about people's experiences in their places of work. He discovered that many were working 12-hour shifts in the nearby Fownes glove factory or Hardy and Padmore's foundry, and receiving wages that served to keep them at the poverty level. In order to seek to meet their needs, he began to organise soup kitchens and other types of provision, while also coming to the view that the wrongs created by the economic system needed to be addressed at a more fundamental level. Alongside his own personal generosity to those in need (which became well known), he was to continue to develop his thinking about the causes of unjust social and economic structures.

In his early responses to the First World War, Studdert Kennedy echoed the prevailing nationalistic sentiments of much of society and the churches. He stated: 'I cannot say too strongly that I believe every able-bodied man ought to volunteer for service anywhere. There ought to be no shirking of that duty. Those who cannot volunteer for military service can pray.' In December 1915, having made provision for a replacement at St Paul's, he was appointed a Chaplain to the British Forces, and he soon started conducting services and giving pastoral support to troops in France. In the early months of 1916 at Rouen, Normandy, as soldiers stopped for a short time on the way to the Front, he spoke to them in ways that they understood, offered to write letters home if they could not, and gave out New Testaments and packets of Woodbine cigarettes. Other chaplains were engaged in similar ministries, but the impact of Studdert Kennedy was such that he was given a personal designation – 'Woodbine Willie'.

An ability to communicate in a highly effective manner to larger audiences outside church settings, which would be a notable feature of his ICF ministry, was evident when Studdert Kennedy gave Lent talks to troops in 1916. After one in which he presented the message of the cross, there was a moment of silence: then, he wrote, they cheered, 'they roared, and their roar was in answer to the call of Christ'. He reworked these messages as the book, *Rough Talks of a Padre* (1918). Front-line duties followed in 1916–18. His asthma, an existing condition, was aggravated by being gassed. At Messines Ridge, in 1917, he volunteered to go and get morphine when the medical centre ran out. He did so under constant bombardment. Having returned with morphine, he went out again to rescue three wounded soldiers. For this 'conspicuous gallantry and dedication to duty', he was awarded the Military Cross. At one stage during his chaplaincy ministry, Studdert Kennedy became part – though somewhat reluctantly – of the Church of England's National Mission for Repentance and Hope. His developing ministry began to include poetry writing. In the poems, the speakers were often soldiers or grieving mothers or wives: through presenting these, Studdert Kennedy wanted to articulate serious questions. His *Rough Rhymes* appeared in 1918 and was very widely read.

One of Studdert Kennedy's most important books (he was to produce several in the 1920s), *The Hardest Part*, was also published in 1918. This covered substantial themes: nature, history, the Bible, democracy, prayer, the sacraments, the Church and life eternal. At the heart of the book was a desire on the part of Studdert Kennedy to write, as Archbishop Michael Ramsey observed in his own commendation, 'for readers sensitive to the agonies of the world'. In it, Ramsey said, God was portrayed as 'the greatest sufferer of all'. By now, Studdert Kennedy was outspoken in his condemnation of war. He described talk of 'the glory of war' as 'utter blather'. War was only 'glorious', he continued, 'when you buy it in the *Daily Mail* and enjoy it at your breakfast table'. In reality it was 'damnable brutality'.

In many ways, this change of tone, so evidently different to the naïve cleric who urged his parishioners to head for the Western Front and then followed in their wake, represents not only Studdert Kennedy's personal journey, but the emerging consciousness of the wartime generation. Those whose life circumstances left them with no real choice but the squalor and poverty of a Worcester factory worker, were now being sent headlong into enemy gunfire at the bidding of the same classes who had once profited through their labour. The consensus that previously led people to simply accept this as their lot was beginning to crumble, and Studdert Kennedy was not alone in seeking to tear down the facades of glory and success that sustained it.

A poem 'Waste' written in 1919 expresses his feelings about both war and the relentless pursuit of profit for the few:

> Waste of muscle, waste of brain
> Waste of patience, waste of pain
> Waste of manhood, waste of health
> Waste of beauty, waste of wealth
> Waste of blood and waste of tears
> Waste of youth's most precious years
> Waste of ways the saints have trod
> Waste of glory, waste of God
> War

Studdert Kennedy also began to articulate his developing understanding of God, in the light of the horrors of what he had experienced. He was equally committed to challenge any religious gloss that might serve to defend this status quo. He was adamant: 'I don't believe there is an absolute Almighty Ruler'. He could not see how anyone could believe that. In the aftermath of the war, Studdert Kennedy was a pioneer in portraying a suffering God and in challenging accepted understandings of the nature of divine power.

Finding a new role

In March 1919, Studdert Kennedy returned to St Paul's, Worcester, but he
was now nationally known as an author, a holder of the Military Cross and
(following the Armistice) a King's Chaplain, and it was likely that he would
move on to a wider role. He continued to write, working late into the night
on this task, after a full day of parish involvement in which his pastoral
work with individuals was intense. After some services at St Paul's there
were up to a hundred people wanting to see him. Several of his articles
about the pervasive disillusionment and restlessness at the end of the war
were collected in the book, *Lies!* (1919). Here he attacked common lies such
as the view that people are only animals, that conflict between classes is
inevitable, that Marxism offers an economic solution and – once more – that
war has the power to uplift. For him the years of war were 'a perpetual horror
chamber'. At root, for Studdert Kennedy, there was a need to recognise that
sin was the stumbling block preventing social reconstruction.

There is much more that could be said about this celebrated chaplain
who returned from the horrors of the Western Front, but in the brief sketch
above, there is enough to detect that Studdert Kennedy showed himself
to be an ideal person to fulfil the vision that P. T. R. Kirk had for ICF. The
narrative above explains something of why Studdert Kennedy was such
a compelling orator, but the simple truth was that he could always be
guaranteed to muster a crowd, and if ICF were to communicate its vision
beyond the corridors of power and influence, few could be more suited
to the task. But it is important to note that Kirk perceived something far
deeper than simply drawing on his deserved reputation in some kind of
inter-war equivalent of celebrity endorsement. The reason that Studdert
Kennedy had adapted so easily to the initially unfamiliar context of military
service was because he tenaciously refused to be anything other than the
person he had always been. His ministry to the troops and his anger at
their plight was rooted in a genuine love for them as God's creation and
a dogged determination to make sense of faith in the face of any situation
he faced, qualities he had already shown in his previous curacies. He
could be completely at home in another's surroundings yet at almost the
same time appear distinctly out of place because he never sought to be
anything but himself. His acts of gallantry, his unfaltering compassion,
his roughshod rhymes and his fearless oratory were in his eyes nothing
particularly remarkable – he was simply embracing whatever reality faced
him. At a time when ICF had yet to fully discover the pathways it would
need to lay if its vision were to become reality, such a temperament was

crucial in plotting their course. And as we trace the journey he helped the newly formed organisation to take, we recognise the many qualities that he brought to it.

Kirk and Studdert Kennedy had similar backgrounds: Anglo-Irish roots, parish ministry in England and chaplaincy during the war. Kirk invited Studdert Kennedy to speak in 1920 at an ICF meeting in St Martin-in-the-Fields church, London, and in the same year it was agreed by ICF to approach him about becoming a 'Messenger' (later often referred to as 'Special Messenger') of the Fellowship. At one of the early ICF crusades, held in Derby in 1921, he and Miss E. Caroline Knight-Bruce were the two principal speakers and they addressed 3,000 people. Knight-Bruce was to be a well-known ICF speaker, described in the 1930s as addressing meetings with her 'accustomed fire'. She and Studdert Kennedy shared a deep concern about the Kingdom of God in relation to areas of social injustice. In 1921, Studdert Kennedy published *Democracy and the Dog Collar*, his most explicitly political volume. This is in the form of a lively dialogue between two men: Mr Organised Labour and Mr Organised Christianity. The conversational format suited Studdert Kennedy well, since he was at home speaking to audiences in which there were doubters, objectors and hecklers. His main speeches were meticulously prepared and memorised, but he also relished debate. In the book, part of his aim was to challenge the Church of England on some important social and economic issues and at the same time to advocate co-operation – between classes in society, management and workers, and Labour and the Church.

Although Studdert Kennedy was known for his ability to communicate to those outside the churches, he also looked for ways to ensure that faith within the churches was firmly grounded. One of his publications in the early 1920s was *Food for the Fed-Up* (1921), an enigmatic title for what was a serious and sustained theological exposition (316 pages) of the Apostles' Creed. In accepting the invitation from ICF to work for the Fellowship, he was keen to find a way to continue a pastoral and parish ministry. In 1922, he moved from St Paul's, Worcester, and was installed as Rector of St Edmund's, Lombard Street, in the City of London. This parish provided him with an income alongside what ICF could afford. His family – he and Emily had three sons – remained in Worcester. St Edmund's was in the financial district of London and it was reckoned that Studdert Kennedy's duties on Sundays would be light, since few people lived in the area. However, his preaching soon attracted large crowds. He conducted an 8.30 a.m. Holy Communion service and invited communicants to breakfast afterwards. Two further services often took place, at 11.00 a.m. and 6.30 p.m. The church building was not large, and it was known for people to begin queuing at 4.30 p.m. for the 6.30 p.m. Evensong.

As already observed, his role in ICF was an outworking in wide-ranging ways of what he discovered as a parish priest and a chaplain. He believed that the Christian faith addressed the challenges of every context, but that the message should never be communicated in a simplistic or naïve fashion. The talks he gave across the country on behalf of ICF were often suffused with Christian apologetic, but as is clear in his *Food for the Fed-Up*, this was accessible and indeed spicy in its style. He aimed at those who were 'fed-up' with what they saw as superficial religion, with the horrors of war and with the false optimism of the period after the First World War. He saw the historic creeds of the Church as providing a framework in which life was given a purpose. Ultimately, he wanted people to find a better way than the way of disillusionment. As he said, 'We must have a creed, a symbol of our faith in this world's final meaning and purpose, or we shall become "fed-up" with life.' The symbol he saw as central, and which he argued was a reality, was the suffering God. The heart of the creed was God in Christ, God as immanent. It was because of the belief in the presence of God in the world that there was the possibility of seeing evil overcome. This message was, as he saw it, highly relevant to the world of the 1920s which he was addressing.

Spiritual resources

The picture sometimes painted of Studdert Kennedy is of a person of unremitting activism. It is true that in his ICF work he was often travelling to public events. However, he was also often asked to lead retreats and to speak about spiritual resources. For him, this was essential to the life of ICF. *The Wicket Gate* (1923), which of all his books was probably the most read, was framed around the Lord's Prayer. In it he wrote that he wanted spiritual life that 'feeds upon constant prayer and communion with God'. A contemporary reviewer of the book wrote: 'In the opening chapter a really striking picture of the perplexities of our time is given, under the figure of Bunyan's pilgrim desperately looking hither and thither for some way of escape from the city of Destruction, and dimly perceiving the light which shines above the Wicket Gate.' At the time, John Bunyan's *Pilgrim's Progress* was still widely known to the general public. What he did was to take the picture of the Gate, and rework it to offer a way into spiritual experience. The book was, as Studdert Kennedy put it, 'plain bread' (the subtitle of the book) for people he encountered as he spoke around England. In the foreword, he said that 'there is scarcely a page of it which is not an attempt to answer questions put to me in conversation after meetings'. Two years later (in 1925), *The Word and the Work* appeared, a series of meditations for Lent.

There were several important perspectives in Studdert Kennedy's approach to spirituality. One was that the spiritual person was a fully human person – not superhuman. He wrote in *The Wicket Gate*: 'Religion leaves a million questions unanswered and apparently unanswerable.' The purpose of faith, he continued, was not to make someone 'certain and cocksure about everything' but to foster certainty, or assurance, about things that were necessary to 'live a human life'. A second important feature for him was that spiritual resources were intimately connected with the world of thought, not simply of feeling. Again, in *The Wicket Gate*, he argued that faith 'does not relieve us from the duty of thought' but rather makes thinking possible.

> It does not put an end to research and enquiry, it gives a basis from which real research is made possible and fruitful of results; a basis without which thinking only means wandering round in circles, and getting nowhere in the end, and research means battering at a brass door that bruises our knuckles, and does not yield by the millionth part of an inch.

Finally, for him, the spiritual life was at odds with the secular agenda, and he was adamant that 'if we allow whole departments of our life to become purely secular, and to create and maintain moral or immoral standards of their own, in time the whole of life is bound to become corrupt'. Whether or not it can be fully attributed to Studdert Kennedy, one legacy of this era is ICF's ongoing commitment to challenge what is sometimes described as the sacred–secular divide.

A powerful medium through which Studdert Kennedy communicated spiritual experience was poetry. He followed up his *Rough Rhymes* with *Songs of Faith and Doubt* (1922) and *The Sorrows of God* (1924). The volume of poems that became his most popular was *The Unutterable Beauty* (1927). The sales of his volumes of poetry reached hundreds of thousands. Studdert Kennedy did not aim for sophistication: rather he wanted to communicate in everyday language to the ordinary person, conveying a message that made a spiritual impression. There were different types of poems in *The Unutterable Beauty*. Although not published until 1927, when he had been involved over several years with ICF work, it included poems shaped by his experience of war. Another type of poem emerged from his wider experiences. Poems such as 'Indifference. When Jesus came to Birmingham' (Matthew 25:31–46), had long-lasting and powerful impact. Studdert Kennedy compares the derided crucified Jesus of first-century Jerusalem with an imagined, ignored, crucified Christ in Birmingham who is left to die alone in the rain. There were also poems using dialects of English (again soldiers featured here), offering reflections on life and faith. Some of what Studdert Kennedy wrote was intended to inspire. For example, 'Solomon in All His Glory' portrayed the ragged uniforms worn by soldiers as more beautiful than Solomon's garments. The inner life shines through the outward, which might not in itself appear glorious. Other poems were marked by a scathing critique of society, such as 'Waste' (see page 51), detailing waste of muscle, brain, patience, pain, manhood, health, beauty and wealth, which Studdert Kennedy linked with the war and economic deterioration.

It was felt to be important in the 1930s that Studdert Kennedy's ministry as a conductor of retreats was not forgotten. William Moore Ede, the Dean of Worcester Cathedral, a supporter of ICF and close friend of Studdert Kennedy, published *The New Man in Christ: A Book of Devotion* (1932). This contained addresses by Studdert Kennedy, several given at High Leigh, Hertfordshire, and some previously unpublished articles. In the addresses, he sought to connect times of retreat with the vision espoused by ICF for Christian impact in society. The 'way of the cross' involved following Jesus and seeking to address human needs. The vision stretched beyond individual renewal to the creation of a world that more fully reflected God's Kingdom. In a series of retreat addresses on the Beatitudes, Studdert Kennedy referred to Julian of Norwich's vision that 'all shall be well' and proposed that 'meekness' was a key spiritual element which could have a role to play in areas such as disarmament and industrial relations. Other themes covered in his retreat meditations included 'John's Gospel', in which he spoke of how the 'I am' sayings of Jesus never 'grated' because they were about 'you', and other titles: 'Easter Day', 'Comprehending the Love of God', 'He Maketh me to Lie Down in Green Pastures' and 'Treasure Upon Earth'. Studdert Kennedy painted on a large spiritual canvas.

A prophetic voice

Passionate preaching in favour of social justice was a widely recognised feature of Studdert Kennedy's ministry. *The Hardest Part*, written in 1918, was described by Jürgen Moltmann, one of the most influential theologians of the second half of the twentieth century, as a work of theology which had 'a prophetic and radical force rather like that of [Karl] Barth's *Epistle to the Romans*, which came out at about the same time'. The following year saw the Versailles Peace Conference, in which the victorious Allied powers imposed harsh treaty terms on their defeated enemies, and Studdert Kennedy took the view that the world was 'a bigger muck up after the peace conference than before'. In his poem 'Dead and Buried', he called the treaty a 'sweet and scented lie'. Although ICF was not a pacifist movement, Studdert Kennedy's sentiments were similar to those expressed in this period by the pacifist Fellowship of Reconciliation, which described the treaty as 'the absolute negation of the New Testament'. Studdert Kennedy was among those who anticipated, with prophetic insight, the danger that there could be further conflict if reconciliation was not part of the vision for the future.

In statements that Studdert Kennedy made which can be regarded as prophetic there was a strong element of warning. This was not the kind of warning that some preachers of the past had issued about the danger of 'hell-fire' or eternal judgements. Indeed, he stated quite explicitly: 'We can no longer frighten people by the thought of hell-fire. They simply do not believe in it.' However, he was in another sense a prophet of judgement when he asserted that life without God was 'hell'. He also felt that during the war he and others had experienced 'a perpetual torture chamber'. Studdert Kennedy did not believe that living through hell would in itself bring people closer to God. He stated in the early 1920s that there was no great post-war religious revival. War, he declared, did not have the capacity to uplift. Rather, there needed to be a call to embrace an alternative to war. He described the alternative with strong words, such as 'fire', 'wrath' and 'love', and linked his vision with the prophetic tradition. Thus, in *The Wicket Gate*, he wrote:

> If the Church is to be a Church indeed, and not a mere farce – and a peculiarly pernicious farce, a game of sentimental make-believe – she must be filled to overflowing with the fire of the ancient prophets for social righteousness, with the wrath and love of the Christ.

Some of Studdert Kennedy's rhetoric seemed to point in the direction of socialist solutions. There was a focus on pressing social issues during the coal strike, followed by the national strike, of 1926. In one of his 1926 speeches, as reported by the *Church Times*, Studdert Kennedy stated in forthright terms: 'I hate living in a world where there is a nice end of town where presumably all the nice people live and an end of dirty ramshackle pigsties where apparently all the nasty people live.' Such assessments produced a negative reaction to ICF from some clergy. The Archdeacon of Chester, William Paige Cox, commented that the objects of ICF were 'excellent, and it was started under promising auspices; but its operations have been conducted in such a partisan way that many of the clergy will now have nothing to do with it.' Studdert Kennedy believed that the prophetic at times had to be partisan, but he denied that what he said implied socialism: 'Not a single one of the ICF activities,' he insisted,

> has fallen under the control of socialists. If any of them did I would sever my connexion with the Society immediately. I am not a Socialist, and spend a considerable amount of my time exposing popular Socialist clap-trap, which is a curse to sane thinking, as popular Tory clap-trap is on the other side. Bother them both.

Further, it was made clear that it was 'a direct contradiction of the aim of the Fellowship [ICF] to associate the Church with a particular policy'.

Those who worked most closely with Studdert Kennedy within ICF all saw his ministry as prophetic. He embodied and articulated a message that they believed the Church – perhaps especially the Church of England – needed to hear. Studdert Kennedy's vivid statements captured this message. The Church was not 'the Ark of Salvation' for those within, but 'the Agent of Salvation' for the whole world. The call was 'not security, but sacrifice', which was 'the hallmark of the Cross'. In prophetic vein, Studdert Kennedy spoke about sin: the sin 'of our modern slums, and the degradation that they cause'; of 'our over-crowded, rotten houses, and the ugliness and vice they bring'; of 'unemployment, with the damnation of body and soul that it means to men and women, boys and girls'; and of 'heartless, thoughtless luxury at one end, standing out against the squalid and degrading poverty at the other'. He never forgot, or allowed others to forget, 'the sin of war, the very sin of sins, which is but the bursting into a festering sore of all the filth that the others have bred in years of miscalled peace'. One author, Linda Parker, coined the term 'Shellshocked Prophets' in her analysis of the way former First World War chaplains such as Studdert Kennedy and Philip Clayton addressed inter-war issues, often bringing the insights from their own experiences. For Studdert Kennedy, a radical message needed to be heard by the Church, and if this was not taken to heart 'then the Church is not a Church at all; and no amount of organization, propaganda, and evangelization can make it live. It has missed its vocation.'

A team member

The team of people with whom he worked in ICF was very important to Studdert Kennedy. He dedicated *The Wicket Gate* to P. T. R. Kirk and the staff at ICF's Fellowship House, 'together with all my comrades and colleagues in that great work', and he spoke of their 'enthusiasm and unfailing friendship'. The encouragement was two-way. The ICF team across the country greatly appreciated Studdert Kennedy's generosity, spiritual insight, humour and compassion. Studdert Kennedy had a vision for what ICF fellowship could be and do, but his vision extended much more widely. He appreciated the work of Philip Thomas Byard Clayton CH MC FSA, 'Tubby' Clayton (who set up Toc H, a society for ex-soldiers in 1919, receiving its Royal Charter in 1922). Clayton had helped to set up a rest house for soldiers called Talbot House at Ypres, which became known to the troops as Toc H (after the phonetic signalling code used by the Army), and which after the war became an international Christian organisation. Studdert Kennedy explored ways in which ICF's ministry could be extended internationally, and he did travel beyond Britain – twice to North America – but his strength was ministry in contexts that he knew well.

As well as preaching in St Edmund's, where he was Rector, Studdert Kennedy was also closely connected with St Martin-in-the-Fields, Trafalgar Square, London, where H. R. L. (Dick) Sheppard was the inspirational vicar. From 1919 to 1929, Studdert Kennedy contributed regularly to Sheppard's parish magazine and Sheppard would advise people to arrive early when Studdert Kennedy preached if they were going to get a seat in the church. In 1924, Sheppard broadcast the first-ever church service on the BBC, and his broadcast sermons and later his Peace Pledge Movement gave him national fame. Studdert Kennedy did not live to see the growth of the pacifist movement in the 1930s, but his view of war affected close friends such as Sheppard. When a book was produced about Studdert Kennedy by his friends, Sheppard was one of the contributors, alongside several others including J. K. Mozley, Warden of St Augustine's House, Reading, who was an early close friend, William Temple and Kirk.

In the contribution William Moore Ede made to this book, he described the approach of Studdert Kennedy (this referred especially to his Worcester ministry but also more widely) as that of 'an Evangelical at heart who loved and lived by the Catholic way of discipline and worship'. This illustrates well the way in which Studdert Kennedy saw the Christian witness, in the workplace and elsewhere, as transcending ecclesial boundary lines. He wanted unity among Christians and saw this as 'the essence of Catholicism'.

For him the Catholic tradition, which he affirmed, was not about 'rituals' or 'ceremonies' in worship. Rather, he argued, 'Catholicity is to respond to the call of God to bear the sin of the whole world, and consecrate every department of life to Jesus Christ'. In writing on 'God and the Sacrament', he stated in typically provocative fashion that the real duty of a 'good Catholic' was not to 'wear vestments and hate Nonconformists' but instead 'to love everybody and wear Christ'. He spoke of learning from Nonconformists about preaching. His deeply felt wish was that all branches of the Christian Church should 'go out together in the power of the Suffering God, speaking a simple Gospel with tongues of flame, and bearing a simple Sacrament with hands that tremble for the precious thing they hold'. In *The Word and the Work*, he portrayed the Christian community as 'a new quality of social life', which was 'redemptive'.

The study and research aspects of ICF's work – inherited from the Christian Social Union – were areas to which Studdert Kennedy contributed. He was known to miss train connections on his incessant travels because he was so absorbed in reading a book. One ICF aim was to 'set up Christ as the teacher'. Among Studdert Kennedy's major interests were evolutionary science, the social sciences and psychology, all of which he saw as part of the reality of God's world. He affirmed engagement with science, arguing that many early scientists had been motivated by seeing God in creation. He interpreted evolution as change which entailed death, associating that with the concept of sacrifice. In the field of the social sciences he explored the journey of finding the true self and of human purpose, which was to be found in knowing God and in serving what he called the 'other-self' or community. He contrasted this sense of purpose with the atheistic view of humanity. Finally, Studdert Kennedy immersed himself in the developing thinking in psychology, including the 'New Psychology'. He was fascinated by the perspectives of Freud and Jung in relation to Christian faith, and his last major work, *The Warrior, The Woman and the Christ* (1928), was a psychological study of the suffering and sacrificial self in which he saw Jesus, the exemplar, as combining male and female qualities.

Studdert Kennedy, along with other ICF messengers, might well be described as an example of what we identify as 'pioneer ministers' in today's Church. Those who believe themselves to be called to this vocation might find some valuable lessons within the example that he offers. Reflecting on this incredible life of service, three crucial strands emerge that combined to make him the person that he was.

The first is quite simply that he was not afraid to inhabit the reality of those to whom he was called to minister. Whether his deliberate choice of parishes in areas of deprivation, or his willingness to venture into no man's land or to engage in rigorous debate, he was committed to a ministry that seriously engaged at the front line; what many describe as an utter devotion to those for whom he ministered. As he advised one aspiring military chaplain:

> Live with the men, go where they go, make up your mind that you will share all their risks and more… work in the very front, and they will listen to you when they come out to rest, but if you only preach and teach behind, the men won't pay the slightest attention to you. The men will forgive you anything but a lack of courage and devotion.

This is an attitude that shaped his ministry throughout, seeing it not as a retreat into a spiritual or religious realm but as a call to engage in the everyday life of those he aspired to serve. He recognised the issues that people faced there, spoke the language that people understood there, and sought to develop and share an understanding of the Gospel that was rooted in that reality. Even in his writing, he considered his task not so much to somehow explain the narratives of religion to the masses but to articulate the experience of the masses to the religious. This he explains profoundly in the post-script to his book *The Hardest Part*.

Few will be gifted with the eloquence that Studdert Kennedy was able to display, but we are unwise to ignore his example of seeking to engage constantly in dialogue between the narratives of our faith and the challenges that our world presents. In many respects his speaking, writing and poetry were the compelling evidence of that deeper task. For all his relentless vigour, he was no mindless activist, but constantly sought to be rooted in careful and thorough reflection on the creeds and Scriptures of his faith.

A second strand to note is that Studdert Kennedy saw the task of the Church, and therefore his own task, as making a real and effective response to the realities he faced. On his arrival in Worcester, prior to his days with ICF, he set up soup kitchens and after-school clubs to address the evident need and poverty that confronted him. He was also a man who practised what he preached; the Chaplain to the King who was able to speak and write so powerfully on issues of injustice, is the same Studdert Kennedy that we meet on the balcony of an inner-city tenement, struggling to drag his bedframe up the stairs to the house of someone he perceived as in greater need of it than himself. He was a man who took the call to mission of 'Word made flesh' seriously, often living it out at significant personal cost. Many of his contemporaries argued that it was impossible to know him fully through his writings alone; these were inseparable from a personality that was shot through with the causes and concerns that he espoused. Those who would be heralds of Good News in any era, need to live and breathe that which they proclaim.

And the third element to note was his concern to speak and act in ways that challenged the underlying causes of the crucial issues that concerned him. Whether it was the social inequalities to which the tenements of Leeds and Worcester bore testimony, or the propensity for war that cost the lives of thousands in the trenches, Studdert Kennedy saw beyond immediate circumstances to challenge the systems and structures that created them. It is perhaps this aspect of his ministry that bound him most to the work and vision of ICF. Among its ranks were key influencers and decision-makers from the worlds of religion, politics and industry, and though at times his words were difficult and unpalatable, no one could question the integrity of spirit with which they were spoken. He was able to speak truth to power, not only because of his God-given wit and eloquence, but because he lived a life that was rooted in the lives of those whose cause he advocated, and it was always their interests and not his own that he sought to pursue.

Yet within that, he never lost sight of the fact that he was first and foremost a minister of the Gospel. His message was driven not by the despair of the realities before him, but his inescapable vision of a better world, revealed through a proper understanding of the teachings of the Christ he loved, and in whose name he loved others. While political causes may have resonated with much of what he had to say, he remained rooted in his identity as a follower of Jesus. Whatever end he sought to achieve, he and his fellow ICF messengers were never tempted by expediency to abandon their sense of impartiality and faith identity.

These three remain the core elements of incarnational mission to this day, just as they can be detected in the work of the Navvy Mission that preceded the ICF era. To be fully rooted in the communities that we are called to serve, engaging with others in addressing the needs that we meet and articulating the cause of the oppressed to those with power to bring about change.

Such mission does not come without significant personal cost and, in Studdert Kennedy's case, this reality was exacerbated by his recklessly selfless personality. His years serving ICF were exhausting. He often came to a speaking engagement struggling with asthma. He would then deliver one of his remarkable messages, but would later suffer collapse. In March 1929, he travelled to Liverpool to give a series of Lenten talks. On 8 March, he was speaking at St Catherine's church, Liverpool, but began to show symptoms of flu. His asthma set in, his heart began to fail, and his wife was sent for and arrived. He died later that day in St Catherine's vicarage. St Catherine's was filled for a requiem 24 hours after his death and 2,000 people visited the church. His body was then taken to Worcester, stopping on the way for impromptu services requested mostly by working men. Studdert Kennedy was buried in Worcester, with thousands of people lining the streets during the funeral procession. Wreaths were sent from all over the country, including one from the King and Queen as well as many that indicated the senders were working men and women. One friend, Charles Raven, who was soon to become Regius Professor of Divinity at Cambridge, said: 'We let him work himself to death; he gave his life for us.' A memorial plaque erected in Worcester Cathedral spoke of Studdert Kennedy as 'A poet; A prophet; A passionate seeker after truth; An ardent advocate of Christian fellowship.'

Reflection: a model of Christian discipleship

If we were to describe Studdert Kennedy in terms familiar to theology today, we would describe him as an early presenter of liberation theology. He was a pioneer of the portrayal of the suffering God and a Gospel for the poor. He challenged social injustice and unjust economic systems, while remaining steadfast in his love for Christ and the vision of the Church as the agent of salvation.

For Studdert Kennedy in his ministry, it was always the case of orthopraxis alongside orthodoxy as seen in his poem 'Indifference' inspired by Matthew 25:31–46. The central ICF concern with faith and work and of being attentive to faith issues in the workplace are found in Studdert Kennedy's ministry and writings.

His concerns for the people to whom he ministered grew with his emerging consciousness of the brutality of war, experienced as he lived and shared the life of the soldiers in the trenches. He reflected on the unjust economic system and commented that the poor were sent into enemy gunfire by the classes that profited from their labour in the factories. Yet he was at pains to point out that he was not a socialist, but rather a follower of Christ and his agenda. Salvation addressed the sin of slums and unemployment and should address and challenge the causes of social injustice.

Like Jesus, accompanying the two disciples on the road to Emmaus (Luke 24:13–35), Studdert Kennedy walked alongside people, engaging in everyday life. He was prophetic in bringing the experience of the masses to the attention of the Church, and he lived the message of salvation for the poor that he proclaimed.

Studdert Kennedy was concerned about poverty, local and worldwide, the value and worth of women and children, sexual equality, and a fairer world and society. He was a social evangelist, who while rejoicing in conversions to the faith, had a wider content to his evangelism. He gave prominence to how Christianity should be lived, the welcoming of working-class people into churches, the practice of proper sexual relationships, the ethics used by employers and employees, the relief of unemployment and poverty, and the condemnation of war. The whole Gospel for Studdert Kennedy consisted of how people should relate to God and to society.

He was a man of courage and outspoken integrity, publicly acclaimed as a selfless pastor, fearless prophet and inspiring preacher. It is impossible not to be inspired and challenged by the life of this imitator of Christ.

This is at the core of the mission that ICF seeks to support today.

Chapter 4

The Fellowship and a new order

The structure and shape of any organisation, including those founded in pursuit of Christian mission, will be a combination of three core elements: its underlying aims and purposes; the personalities and vision of its key individuals; and the prevailing circumstances and context within which it operates. As The Industrial Christian Fellowship (ICF) entered the 1930s, there is no doubt that one of those elements was significantly impacted by the untimely death of Studdert Kennedy. It is impossible to know the degree to which the organisation was shaped around his unique character, or what should be attributed to the providence of its ideal advocate emerging at a crucial moment, but what cannot be denied is that, to this day, ICF is imbued with the values and vision that he so vehemently advocated.

This was a period in which the Fellowship continued to be involved in a number of discussions about the future direction of British society. New influences began to affect its work, while at the same time, many of the activities which had characterised it in the previous decade continued. Engagement with what could be termed 'public theology' was at times controversial. In the later 1930s, there were accusations that the Fellowship, with its strong stress on the need for a new social order, was advocating 'some form of economic collectivism' as necessary for 'social salvation'. This is worth noting, as it may also be a subtle reflection of a shift in emphasis that had taken place in the first decade of its life. Earlier controversies took for granted its engagement in public life and largely revolved around whether its ideas were too closely aligned with emerging socialist and communist thought. Concern now began to revolve more around whether it was neglecting the salvation of souls in pursuit of issues of social justice.

In the midst of a number of public claims and counter-claims about ICF's work, C. S. Woodward, Bishop of Bristol and its Chair, was emphatic that 'the new order we hope for', from a Christian point of view, could emerge only 'if the soul of the individual and of the nation is redeemed by the living power of Christ'. In the light of that, he argued that specific political proposals for reform or reconstruction were to be judged by their ability to encourage 'a corporate change of mind' and that this was 'a religious and not a political judgment'. This chapter looks at the developments in the 1930s and the way in which these contributed to the significant Malvern Conference of 1941.

New influences

With the death of Studdert Kennedy in 1929, P. T. R. Kirk looked for those he knew who might be able to accompany him in giving a lead to the Fellowship. While Studdert Kennedy might have been its public face, Kirk's constant attention to embedding his work, along with others, in an effective organisational network should not be underestimated. He took heart from the fact that 30 diocesan bishops had affirmed the role of ICF and had stated that it would be 'disastrous' if its enterprise was curtailed. This gave Kirk the impetus he needed to seek new advocates for its work, but they too would stamp their own mark on its work.

To consider the impact of that, we might return briefly to Lionel Hitchens. A comparison between him and Studdert Kennedy reveals two individuals aligned in common accord but coming from very different foundations. Studdert Kennedy was very much the advocate for the ordinary people, many of whom had borne the brunt of prevailing social injustices, while Hitchens sought the same ends from the perspective of a successful diplomat and industrialist. It is testimony to Kirk's ingenuity and the Fellowship's depth of engagement that such an outspoken critic of war could co-exist with a trustee who had risen to prominence on the back of British imperialism and played such a key role in the production of armaments. What is less clear is whether Kirk was motivated more by the kind of evangelistic zeal exemplified by Studdert Kennedy or the vision of a society defined by the values of the Kingdom of God that might validly define Hitchens' motivation. Perhaps this was because Kirk genuinely saw the two as interdependent and his key vision was to create an environment where the two could interact and flourish.

But, as others came to the fore in the wake of Studdert Kennedy's ministry, while ideologically ICF remained unchanged, perhaps one of the things that gave rise to the criticisms that the Bishop of Bristol was so keen to dispel was a distinct shift in the position of its key public advocates. They may have been able to commend the same vision as Studdert Kennedy, but did so from a much more theoretical platform than the lives and experiences of those whose wellbeing was their common concern.

One of those who became prominent as a writer and speaker for the Fellowship was V. A. Demant. He fitted well, since he was the Director of Research for the inter-church Christian Social Council, which had emerged as a continuation of the Conference on Christian Politics, Economics and Citizenship (COPEC) and which held its meetings at Fellowship House. Demant had embraced the Christian faith and become an Anglican while at university in Oxford and he subsequently trained for Anglican ministry at Ely Theological College. He was widely acknowledged to be a brilliant thinker and became Regius Professor of Moral and Pastoral Theology at Oxford. In 1931, Demant contributed three articles to ICF's *The Torch* on 'Unemployment as a Problem in Christian Sociology'. In the same year, a largely Anglo-Catholic group with which Demant was associated launched a new quarterly journal, *Christendom*, which was subtitled 'A Journal of Christian Sociology', and the name 'Christendom group' came into usage. Kirk had increasing contact with the group's members.

The Christendom group was indebted to an earlier movement, the League of the Kingdom of God (LKG). The LKG convened events and by the early 1930s these had evolved into large 'Christendom' conferences held each year at the Mirfield Community's house at 'Moreton', St Leonards-on-Sea, Sussex. Kirk became part of the Christendom group, although for others in ICF, the Christendom movement's conferences and its journal, which was edited and largely financed by Maurice Reckitt, a wealthy Anglo-Catholic layman, had limitations. Discussions within the group, whose members included for example T. S. Eliot, were largely at a high intellectual level. The movement also drew ideas of a Christian society partly from the medieval Church and this perspective tended towards hierarchical societal thinking. ICF's commitment to outreach among those in working life did not sit easily with these views. Indeed, the topics addressed by the Christendom group in lectures at conferences, and in articles and reviews of books published in their journal, were often of little relevance to ICF's work.

However, there were issues which Demant in particular spoke and wrote about which were relevant. He produced a book in 1932, *This Unemployment: Disaster or Opportunity?* (published by SCM Press), in which he expounded at greater length the ideas he had explored in *The Torch* about a Christian response in a time of depression and high unemployment. These included the possibility (known as 'social credit') that there should be payment to the unemployed as well as wage earners, in order to enhance overall buying power and help stimulate the economy. William Temple, who since 1929 had been the very influential Archbishop of York, was interested in such social policies and had links with Demant and the Christendom group, although he did not accept the medievalist dimension. The ICF Executive encouraged involvement in these developments, especially given Temple's positive regard for Kirk. In this period, ICF was beginning to organise more conferences, particularly for the Anglican clergy, under the auspices of what was named its 'Clergy Fellowship'. Demant spoke at one of these on the subject of 'the present economic deadlock'.

ICF rightly saw the need for a Church that could respond to the opportunities it perceived and it was imperative therefore for Anglican movements which shared a concern for social issues to work together as far as possible. Kirk recognised that the Christendom group, despite its limitations, had intellectual resources to offer, notably through its leaders. In addition to Demant and Reckitt, the other influential figures were Percy Widdrington, an Anglican priest and theologian, Ruth Kenyon, who had been involved in COPEC and was on the Research Committee of the Christian Social Council and the ICF Executive, and W. G. Peck, who would devote his considerable energies to the Fellowship. To balance this group, Kirk made contact with representatives of other Anglican groups, such as the 'liberal evangelical' Anglican Evangelical Group Movement (AEGM), within which Charles Raven was a significant figure. When Raven spoke in Cambridge at a conference, ICF was represented, and strengthened its existing links with St Matthew's Church, which was seeking to reach into one of the poorer districts of Cambridge. The aim was always to seek ways to influence Church thinking on social, industrial and economic questions. Sidney Dark, Editor of the *Church Times* during most of the inter-war period, was strongly supportive of Kirk's vision. The Lambeth Conference of 1930, speaking of social problems, had said little more than that the 'strange paradox' of poverty in the midst of plenty called for 'hard thinking and courageous action'. Kirk hoped to supply what the Lambeth Conference had said was needed.

Taking action

The translation of ideas into action was Kirk's particular strength and there is no doubt that he played a crucial role in equipping particularly the Anglican Church to play its part in the vision around which ICF had been founded. But through his endeavours, we can also trace an increasing drift towards an organisation preoccupied and defined by ecclesial concerns and less directly engaged in public life. This, as much as anything, might be detected by observing that it was bishops rather than public figures who increasingly appear as its key advocates, and indeed much of the criticism which they addressed came either from within the Church or centred around religious issues. This might be the outcome of a strong episcopal representation in its hierarchies from the outset, or the fact that during its first decade other movements gained momentum. The Labour Party and trade unions would be the most obvious of these, where many of the values that they and ICF had in common could be pursued, often by individuals whose vision was nonetheless undergirded and informed by a strong Christian faith. Many were happy to remain in membership and be advocates of ICF, but it was becoming more of a valued narrator, often able to bring moral and religious affirmation to the endeavours of others, and less of a participant outside the confines of the Anglican Church.

In 1931, Kirk became Honorary Secretary of the Church of England's Social and Industrial Commission and it was through his initiative that a standing committee was set up to seek to ensure that there was progress between its sessions. The full Commission also began to meet more frequently and conferences were held at Fulham Palace. In addition to Kirk, several other members of the ICF Executive became involved. The Commission came to be shaped by the social message and the resources that the Fellowship offered. As an example of the impact, the Executive was pleased to record in 1935 the fact that the Church Assembly (which in 1970 was to be replaced by the General Synod) had largely accepted the Social and Industrial Commission's report on unemployment, with its call to address 'disorder' in the social and economic system. Kirk's role in this was pivotal. Following the Assembly's commitment, he wrote to all 700 Assembly members to commend to them ICF's literature and wider expertise as the Church of England addressed the issue of what he called 'islands of depression and hopelessness amid the rising tide of prosperity'. Kirk campaigned around the country, urging the need for economic investment. ICF also supported schemes to provide housing and opportunities for the unemployed.

ICF's 'crusades' or missions continued in this period. In 1933, Geoffrey Fisher, then Bishop of Chester and later Archbishop of Canterbury, was one of the speakers at a major crusade in Birkenhead, Merseyside. Two years later, in Wearmouth, very large meetings as well as many smaller ones for specific groups were held during a 12-day ICF crusade. The largest event attracted 3,000 people to the Empire Theatre, Sunderland, with thousands more in an overflow. The theatre orchestra played and part of the evening was broadcast by the BBC. The smaller meetings were for groups such as the unemployed, factory workers, teachers, doctors, nurses, young people and those interested in sports. Debates with 'secularists' attracted interest. A crusade was not a stand-alone ICF event (or a 'flash in the pan', as some alleged) but was linked with ongoing mission. An example of longer-term work in the North East was an ICF welfare centre in Jarrow. An old paper mill was turned into a club and a workshop and J. L. Greening, an ICF missioner, was the manager. The club had 2,000 members, many of whom were shipyard workers or miners. The workshop offered training in skills for the unemployed, including furniture making, metal work and boot repair. In 1938, the effects of the Merseyside crusade were still being felt.

Although Kirk was a pioneer, he also relied on a dedicated team of activists around him. For most of the 1930s, there were six Area Directors who had a strategic role and also supervised the still large (although reducing) network of lay missioners. One of the Area Directors, T. Dyfan Thomas, whose area was the English Midlands, gave a review of two months of his ministry, which showed what was typically involved. He had spoken at two prisons, three public schools, the Cambridge University Student Christian Movement, a teachers' training college, a diocesan youth camp and an unemployed camp. He had travelled 4,000 miles. In a period when the North-West Area was without a Director, he had covered that as well, but was glad when John Clifford Gill, who had been Rector of an Anglican parish in Glasgow, was appointed. The Area Directors were often those who had strategic responsibility for ICF outreach in their regions. What was done depended on local contexts. In the Rhondda, for example, which had the highest rate of unemployment in England and Wales, there was an emphasis on clubs for the unemployed. By contrast, in Leicester talks about the Christian faith and social issues were a priority, as these attracted large audiences.

There were local ICF branches across the country, with many volunteers organising events. Caroline Knight-Bruce was one of the most effective speakers at large events, often speaking to audiences of a thousand or more. The role of Messenger continued for a time: Mary Gamble was a female Messenger. Among other women who were prominent, Alice Charles was the Fellowship's Director of Studies for 20 years and was at the centre of training initiatives which were initially based in a large house, Thedden Grange, near Alton, in Hampshire. Discussions in the 1940s led to ICF becoming part of what was offered through the cluster of colleges in Selly Oak, Birmingham. This included the College of the Ascension, founded by the Anglican Society for the Propagation of the Gospel initially to train female missionaries. ICF resources were supplied to lay missioners and others who were active in parishes and in state and public schools. A quarterly journal or *Review* was produced, which carried substantial articles. One report noted that missioners were seen by clergy as having the ability to communicate with audiences outside the reach of many of their own number. Some missioners, such as George Snowdon, who joined in 1935, went on to ordination training.

While much of the focus of these activities was industrial life in Britain (and especially England), there were also international links. Kirk was keen to foster connections with the international Labour movement, and at one Labour Conference held in Geneva he spoke on the text, 'Happy is that people, whose God is the Lord' (Psalm 144:15, KJV), and spoke of the Kingdom as something which did not exist 'in some distant sphere above the bright blue sky', but rather a society in which all were in fellowship with God and one another. Inevitably, the way in which Kirk and others sought to encourage societal involvement through painting this kind of picture was criticised by some as being unrealistic utopianism. In response, an ICF publication in 1936 contended that it was wrong to allow ideals to be crushed by 'so-called hard facts'. For Kirk, ideals of 'a world at peace', and 'a better social and economic order' were to be taken out of the realm of the impossible, and instead were to be seen as 'the possibilities inherent in the actual facts'.

Public theology

Although ICF had a strong tradition of active outreach, there was a realisation that theological engagement was an important contribution that the Fellowship could make. This emphasis on theological thought was especially in evidence from the mid-1930s. W. G. Peck, who joined the staff as a full-time organiser in 1936 (having been Rector of St John the Baptist, Hulme, Manchester), had an influential role in this development. Towards the end of 1936, the study department reported that 63 local groups had been formed throughout the country. Among these were what were sometimes called 'mixed groups'. These, which met in a number of centres (London, Manchester and Birmingham being prominent), were characterised by what would now be called 'public theology'. Typically, they were composed of economists, industrialists and theologians. One produced a document on 'The Church and the New Economic Order'. This attempted to set out what were seen as principles to be drawn from the theology of the Kingdom of God that were relevant to industry. The current industrial context was assessed against these.

The conferences and 'schools' convened for Anglican clergy, and for ministers of other denominations, which were closely connected to the conferences of the Christian Social Council, were intended during this period to be conduits for the outworking of what was increasingly termed in these circles 'Christian sociology'. ICF was keen to find a consensus among those who saw that social challenges should be brought into the heart of Christian worship. Peck's influence was such that, by the end of the 1930s, about ten major clergy conferences were being convened annually. Up to a hundred could be present. At one conference, the social implications of the Eucharist were examined. It was agreed that this act of Christian worship could never be 'merely individualistic': it was essentially connected to Christian fellowship. Where fellowship was not evident – in Church and in society – this was seen as corporate sin, which called for repentance. Social evils such as slums, sweated labour and war were a breach of fellowship. Out of these deliberations came publications co-sponsored by ICF, on topics such as *War and the Church's Duty* (1937) and *The Church and Monetary Reform* (1939).

As well as seeking to engage existing Anglican clergy and Free Church ministers in the task of formulating public theology, ICF also sought to influence the training of future clergy. Kirk was asked to give evidence on ordination training in the area of Christian sociology before the Archbishops' Commission on Training for the Ministry. Here he was able to draw on much that had been done by ICF since the early 1920s – and even before that by the Christian Social Union – and he presented evidence regarding the need for an approach that equipped clergy theologically and practically for dealing with contemporary industrial society. Kirk was able to show that, to a large extent, such training was lacking but that when ordinands were introduced to these issues – usually by ICF – they came to see this training as vital for their ministries. Kirk also suggested ways by which this could be incorporated into existing training schemes. There was an impact, since in 1938 ICF was able to report that an increasing number of young Anglican incumbents were recognising the service offered by ICF.

The ecumenical dimensions of ICF's work in bringing theological perspectives to bear on wider developments in the world were well illustrated at the Conference on Life and Work held in Oxford in 1937. This was a very significant event in the developing ecumenical movement. The conference delegates analysed the crisis in Europe, with a range of theological views, including pacifism, being articulated. The ICF journal noted that 'the calm deliberation, the confident expectation' that had characterised the previous Life and Work Conference, held in Stockholm in 1925 (which Kirk had attended), had given way to 'tense expectancy, the grim earnestness which marks the throes of conflict'. The reference was to the rise of totalitarian regimes and the threat of war. Knight-Bruce wrote *The Church Speaks* (1938) as an ICF companion to the Oxford papers. This echoed the general thinking from Oxford that the 'menace to Christian culture and civilisation has driven the Church all over the world to consider how it can best deal with a situation which offers it a challenge comparable only to that of the first century.'

This stream of visionary, thoughtful and wide-ranging reflection and learning bears testimony to an organisation that had lost little of the vision with which it was founded. Yet while it was able to do this with clarity within its ever-expanding spheres of influence, what is less evident is that it was able to make this a reality in the public life of the nation.

Issues of identity

The introduction to this chapter suggested three elements that shape the identity of an organisation. We have so far explored ICF's story largely through the personalities and changes in personnel that impacted it during its first two decades. During that period, its ability to defend itself against its critics, and the line of its arguments, further reveal that its underlying purpose and vision had not changed. But it has to be recognised that the society in which this vision was being articulated was also evolving. This, along with the inevitable change in tone of those who articulated that vision, meant that it became expressed and perceived differently with time. This is perhaps illustrated through the debate at the 1938 Church Assembly, introduced by C. S. Woodward, ICF's Chair, calling for its amalgamation with the Social and Industrial Commission. He argued that the Commission would benefit from the use of ICF's 'admirably equipped' headquarters and its paid, full-time staff. It was also clear that he hoped to raise the profile of social questions in the work of the Assembly. Woodward asked if the Assembly were content to be a 'neutral body with no strong views, giving no lead to the Church on great and vital questions'. In the ensuing debate, Woodward's proposal did not gain enough support. The identity of ICF was that of a voluntary body. To unite it with an official Church of England body, it was argued, ran the risk of restricting the freedom it enjoyed and indeed might mean the Fellowship could not take up certain causes with enthusiasm. The other aspect was that the Assembly, which represented the views of the Church of England as a whole, could not be asked to give its approval to all that was said and done by ICF.

The debate in the Church Assembly brought to the fore a number of lay people in the Church of England who had serious reservations. One of these was Charles Marston, an industrialist who was involved in the emerging motor industry and was a Christian philanthropist. He alleged that ICF was becoming involved in promoting collective social remedies when it should be concerned 'to minister to the inner life of the individual'. In reality, Marston was also seeking to promote a social vision, in which Christianity gave support to capitalism. Another critic was J. H. Higginson, a Lecturer at Leeds University and a historian of education in Europe. He referred to a publication, *The Industrial Christian Fellowship: What it Stands For*, in which a statement 'in big black type' was to be found: 'We assert, therefore, that the present order is fundamentally wrong and must be replaced by another and different order.' Like Higginson, Peter Agnew, a Conservative MP who was also a member of the Church Assembly (and would remain until 1965), did not want a new social order but rather reform of any 'particularly flagrant' abuses to be found in the existing system.

This might be seen as testimony to a society that was perhaps less undefined than it was when ICF was first founded almost two decades before. The search for a new social order, at least in the eyes of some, had already given way to a need to reform the one which had emerged (or perhaps had managed to fend off moves for change). The issues outlined in the Old Testament confrontation between Amos and Amaziah became all too clear as the relative merits of influence and liberty were debated. It would seem that, for its critics at least, ICF's vision of a genuine 'fellowship' where the conflicting interests of social, economic and political concerns could amalgamate under the banner of a shared Christian identity had already been abandoned. These causes had other established advocates whose interaction was more one of conflict than one of co-operation. Many, we might say, took these ideologies for granted and were seeking a Christian commentary, if not justification, for them, rather than a vision of Christian identity that commended itself as an alternative.

The responses from the officers of ICF, principally Woodward and Kirk, were robust and sought to underline this. During the debate and in subsequent correspondence in *The Times*, they insisted that the identity of the Fellowship had been misrepresented, pointing out that ICF had always insisted that it stood for 'Christ and His principles', and never offered any particular social or economic scheme as the solution to the human predicament. Rather, the Fellowship's commitment to exploring issues connected with the social order was 'moral, theological, and above all evangelistic'. Kirk challenged anyone to produce any ICF literature that looked at world problems from anything other than that perspective. He argued that this theological position was based on 'the great social traditions of the Church'. Woodward pointed out that *The Industrial Christian Fellowship: What it Stands For* clearly stated that its vision was for 'the Divine Purpose' to be 'the final and determining end' when thinking of social change, and that this change was 'to be effected by the redeeming power of our Saviour Christ'. In speaking of the present order as 'fundamentally wrong', the Fellowship was not espousing a particular collectivist agenda but was maintaining that only a social and economic order which took into account 'spiritual ends' could be affirmed. What currently existed did not address that dimension.

Kirk was right in referring to the 'great social traditions of the Church' in explaining the identity of ICF. William Temple, together with those bishops and clergy in the Church of England who were aware of the challenges of society in the 1930s, did not perceive it as having lost touch with the Christian Gospel. Arthur Winnington-Ingram, Bishop of London, was one of the Anglican leaders who affirmed its ministry. For him, the 'frisky horse' of the Fellowship needed to be free to take risks, rather than being 'too respectable'. Others, such as J. H. Higginson, continued to express great reservations. In a book he produced in 1938, *New Testament Economics*, he dismissed the Christian social tradition. His book was critiqued in the ICF *Review*. The reviewer stated that Higginson had 'armoured himself with a little elementary biblical criticism and his exegesis is as shallow as it is pompous'. Referring to the New Testament reference to the poor having the Gospel preached to them, the reviewer commented: 'There is nothing in Mr Higginson's conception of the Gospel about which the poor could be particularly elated.'

Much of this debate was conducted against the background of the rise of socialist approaches but this did not reflect how ICF was perceived on the ground. Joyce Baines, speaking from a diocesan point of view, concentrated on its evangelistic impact and on ICF-led weeks of retreat in which 'revival was taking place'. Some specific issues that had been of concern to ICF were addressed, such as the significance of the individual in a society characterised by large-scale organisation in industry, finding the balance between the individual and the community, and the need for affordable council housing to be available for working families. Arising out of ICF's Wearmouth crusade, local clergy began holding weekly open-air meetings. The Fellowship was invited to organise the official act of Christian worship at the annual Trades Union Congress (TUC). This had happened before, in the 1920s, with Studdert Kennedy preaching on several occasions. Although the invited preachers typically affirmed the work of the TUC, they also stressed that what was needed in the 'social struggle' was 'spiritual power', or as R. T. Howard, Provost of Coventry (and a leader in the AEGM), put it when speaking at Bridlington in 1939, a vision for a 'New Age'. Above all, ICF's voice was raised in support of the hope that was offered through Christian faith. Hope based on gods such as 'wealth' was ultimately 'doomed'.

The record of these discussions offers a helpful summary of the ongoing activity and vision of ICF, but the context also says a great deal. This was a lively debate within the institutions of the Church of England, and the main subject in focus was ICF itself. Rather than discussing the social order in the light of ICF's espoused vision, it was ICF's vision that was under scrutiny in the light of social order. A subtle but notable shift had taken place that perhaps only hindsight can fully recognise. Yet we can also note the Fellowship's continuing aptitude for bringing key public issues to the fore. The rise of materialism, or the 'god of wealth' as R. T. Howard put it, and the 'corporate sin' of inequality, were being highlighted some decades before they became mainstream issues in public life.

The Malvern Conference and its outcomes

But there is another, more significant, shift in the prevailing context that cannot be ignored. Those who entered the third decade of the twentieth century believed themselves to have done so having put behind them 'the war to end all wars'. Yet as the years progressed this gave way to an increasing concern that was eventually realised, and global conflict once again raised its ugly head. The Second World War seemed to spell the end of hopes that had been raised in the 1930s for British society and ICF alike. Already dented by unrealised promises of a great new order, the generation who grew up in the shadow of this ever-diminishing hope found themselves again enlisted in military conflict.

However, Kirk considered it was important in wartime to think of the future. Perhaps for all the despair that it generated, this might yet represent the opportunity to imagine again the renewed society of which ICF had been such a committed advocate in the years after the previous conflict. He was able to persuade William Temple to be the Chairman of a conference which would draw together Christian thinkers to consider a future post-war social order. Among the speakers he had in mind were T. S. Eliot, Dorothy L. Sayers, W. G. Peck (ICF) and V. A. Demant, who in 1939 wrote *The Religious Prospect*, which ICF found 'a very good book'. These, and others such as John Middleton Murry, Maurice Reckitt and D. M. MacKinnon, accepted invitations to give papers. Kirk and the other staff provided the organisation for the Malvern Conference, so called because it was held at Malvern College. It covered four days, from 7 to 10 January 1941. The conference subject was advertised as 'The Life of the Church and the Order of Society'. Some descriptions have spoken about 400 people being present, but voting figures suggest a lower number. There were 15 bishops, a considerable number of clergy, and 43 deaconesses and other women workers. The object was 'to consider from the Anglican point of view what are the fundamental facts which are directly relevant to the ordering of the new society that is quite evidently emerging, and how Christian thought can be shaped to play a leading part in the reconstruction after the war is over.'

Temple made a number of key points at Malvern. For all the narrative outlined above, he retained his focus on wider society and these points were primarily addressed to those with political power, although in Temple's mind the churches had a crucial part to play in offering a societal vision. As he put it: 'We are here to affirm the right and duty of the Church to lay down principles governing the ordering of society.' He emphasised that the Church as Church laid down principles first of all for individual lives, and did not try to suggest in detail how great corporations should be organised. However, he wanted to state as strongly as possible his belief that in Britain every child should live in a decent family unit, with sufficient food and proper housing; every child should have education until the years of maturity; every citizen should have a decent income; all workers should have a voice in the business or the industry in which they were involved and more widely the opportunity to contribute to the wellbeing of the community; every citizen should have sufficient leisure; and every person should have freedom of worship. In discussion it was noted that perhaps less than 5 per cent of the country was engaged in church-life. Notwithstanding, Temple argued that the business of the Church was to 'infiltrate and leaven' all parts of society.

A spirited debate broke out at Malvern over a resolution proposed by Sir Richard Acland, a Liberal (and later a Labour) MP, which attacked private property and in particular the private ownership of the main industrial resources of the country. An amendment, proposed by George Bell, Bishop of Chichester, was put to the Acland motion. Bell's amendment, which was passed by 75 votes to 60 (with a considerable number of abstentions), did not attack all private property but only situations which had a significantly adverse effect on the poor. A compromise position emerged from this debate. At the end of the conference, Temple drew up a list of conclusions which incorporated things regarded as important, such as the right of the Church to speak into societal issues, the importance of evangelism, the Christian doctrine of humanity and the need for reform in the life and worship of the Church. Societal issues which concerned the conference included the profit motive, unemployment, militarism, the earth's resources and treatment of foreigners. Temple confided in Kirk that he did not want the work done at Malvern to be taken over by the 'political left' as this would alienate many Anglicans. On the reform of the Church, he told Kirk that he did not want Malvern's vision to get into the hands of Anglo-Catholics, with the consequence that 'the Evangelical school will be too little represented and perhaps placed in something like opposition'.

In June 1941, Kirk informed Temple that the Malvern findings, in the form of an ICF pamphlet, had sold nearly 200,000 copies. This was remarkable in such a short space of time and in wartime. Constant reprints followed. Both Temple and Kirk were now talking of a 'movement'. A committee of industrialists, economists and theologians met under Temple's chairmanship to take the movement forward. Further reports were produced and also a bestselling book, *Christianity and the Social Order* (1942), published by Penguin. In this Temple argued – as he had done at Malvern – for a Christian politics which aimed at increasing social equality and improving provision in a number of areas: decent housing, proper education, a living wage, participation in industrial decision-making, working conditions and health, and freedom of worship and of speech.

It might be that, in Temple, ICF had found a public advocate who could attract something of the attention and enthusiasm that was once the domain of Studdert Kennedy, though this would certainly have taken a very different form given his ecclesial office. But once again through untimely death, ICF's prophet was stolen from it. Yet what is perhaps of equal tragedy is that, reading the Malvern pamphlet some 70 years later, much of the economic turmoil, political and banking scandals and other unwelcome features of the early years of the following century are notably predicted in its findings. It is also in the Malvern papers that we find some of the earliest recorded awareness of what would today be described as environmental issues, some decades before they would attract popular consent. It would seem that ICF had lost nothing of its prophetic clarity, yet for all the enthusiasm that surrounded Malvern, it might reasonably be asked whether this was at the expense of real and lasting influence. This was reflected as much by a lack of church attendance at grassroots level as a diminishing representation in the corridors of power. We might also notice that Malvern represents the first serious attempt by ICF to achieve anything resembling an ecumenical or interdenominational representation. Perhaps this move came too late, as Christian identity had already become a far more diverse reality in public life than that which was represented by the almost exclusively Anglican tone of the conference's findings.

For all of this, much that was said by Temple was to be embodied in the welfare state and it was proposed that further follow-up to Malvern would largely be taken on by ICF. It was agreed that staff could commit to this and the point was made that the Fellowship had issued pamphlets on nearly all the subjects considered at the conference. ICF did not, however, underestimate the challenge. C. S. Woodward, Chair of the Council, spoke in 1942 of Anglican confirmations rapidly falling, fewer Sunday school children and local congregations dwindling. But there were encouragements, especially in the proliferation of local cells of Christians of various denominations meeting together. This was advocated at Malvern and was part of ICF life.

Alongside small groups, large meetings were held. Again, ICF took a leading role. During 1942 and 1943, the Malvern agenda was communicated to audiences in several cities. By this time Temple was Archbishop of Canterbury, although his leadership was brought to an end by his premature death in 1944 of a heart attack, at age sixty-three. At an Albert Hall meeting, the main speakers were Temple, Cyril Garbett, who had succeeded Temple as Archbishop of York, and the Labour politician Sir Stafford Cripps, later Chancellor of the Exchequer. The excitement was such that 20,000 people applied for tickets, with many being disappointed. As well as Anglican bishops, leaders from all the Free Churches and from the Roman Catholic and Orthodox Churches attended. Temple's speech attracted most attention. He argued that 'things of the spirit' – knowledge, beauty, courage, love, joy and peace – were to be given primary place. When material things were put first, the result was division and enmity. The profit motive was not wrong in itself but wealth should be shared. He spoke of how the requisites of life – air, light, land and water – could be used well or abused. A Birmingham Town Hall meeting also generated great interest, with a capacity crowd, and audiences in Leicester and Edinburgh were around three thousand. For ICF, these meetings represented a high point. The Fellowship even renamed its quarterly publication, which became the *Malvern Torch*, with the clear intention to continue the work of bringing the 'challenge' of the Malvern Conference.

Press coverage of these events was extensive, and the position of ICF was noted. The *Daily Herald* pointed out the role of Kirk, and said that 20 years earlier Kirk and Studdert Kennedy had been told by some to take their 'social gospel' back to Ireland. This, and the responses that ensued highlight the challenge faced to this day by those who seek to couch their Christian convictions in the narratives and language of contemporary society. Temple was deeply unhappy that the religious parts of his speeches were 'almost invariably omitted' by the press. He wrote to *The Times* to say that in his Albert Hall speech his last point, and in his view his most important point, was that the root trouble was 'the disastrous effects of sin upon social life and the structure of society'. He had said that it was necessary to lead people back to dependence on 'the guidance and strength of God'. The national press had only reported 'political' points, although the Christian newspapers were well balanced in their coverage. Problems continued for Temple. In 1943, he cited a recent speech in which he had insisted that his social proposals would be futile without 'the love of God as proclaimed in the Gospel' and that the fundamental need was 'evangelisation and conversion'. His speech was supplied by the Press Association to every newspaper in England but not one included this part. Temple set up an Advisory Committee of 16 people so that the focus would not be on him: he appointed 'forward-looking people', as he put it, from politics, professions and denominations (although not from industry) such as Cripps, Kirk and George MacLeod of the Iona Community. The hope, as Caroline Knight-Bruce said in a speech at the time, was for a 'new order' in society, and in so doing she echoed those same aspirations with which ICF had been formed in the wake of the previous conflict. It was, however, still a hope that would prove hard to fulfil.

Can we learn?

Steve Turner wrote a poem entitled 'History Lesson' (*Up to Date*, London: Hodder & Stoughton, 1983, p.129):

History repeats itself,
Has to.
No-one listens

As we look back from the early twenty-first century, this period in the life of ICF and wider society generates a disturbing *déjà vu* feeling. So many of the same issues still remain: justice in our society, the gap between rich and poor, economic decisions driven by the global market, gender equality, concerns in the developing world and lack of care for creation. The tragedy is that ICF clearly articulated many of those lessons that were only partially heeded at the time, or that successive generations took a long time to embrace. Time and again, we might make reference to its prophetic voice, raising issues that had reached crisis point before society took serious notice. And many of those crises have been exacerbated by single issues being perceived as in competition rather than dimensions of a wider holistic vision. For ICF, 'Jesus, the Lord of all life' offered a narrative that might have avoided some of the catastrophes that humanity has since encountered.

Temple learned from Reinhold Niebuhr that 'love' in social organisation is 'justice', but he remained optimistic of a top-down social policy. Although Temple, together with R. H. Tawney and William Beveridge, laid down the principles of the 'welfare state' in the early 1940s and especially through the Malvern Conference, only George Bell stood out against the Allied saturation bombing of German cities, and Tawney neglected the place of women and what would then have been termed third world issues.

There is clearly still a role for ICF which is largely unchanged.

Chapter 5

The post-war environment

The far-reaching vision of Malvern and the public interest that it generated gave the Industrial Christian Fellowship (ICF) good reason to anticipate the period after the end of the Second World War with a renewed degree of optimism. Once again society would be in need of reconstruction after a devastating conflict; once again the Fellowship had the ear of key policy-makers and influencers, and through Malvern it had a clear vision with which to move forward. As the end of the conflict drew ever nearer, there was great hope that the Malvern Conference, with its core messages of continuing relevance, would signal the way ahead. It is a measure of this optimism and self-belief that the Malvern Declaration called for 'all Christians to unite in the furthering of these aims'. ICF's vision of an ecumenical Christian community appeared to be one that came together not around ecclesial structures, but a vision for a society of which it would be at the heart. It may have been a further source of optimism for long-standing supporters to read into Temple's introductory statement a belief that the war was a consequence of society's failure to give sufficient attention to the Fellowship's message after the previous conflict. The scale of their vision extended beyond the shores of these islands, looking to a day when this order of life 'would be accepted by rulers and statesmen throughout the British Commonwealth of Nations and would be regarded as the true basis on which a lasting peace could be established'. David Arthur, at the time ICF General Secretary, observed more realistically 50 years later in a 1991 publication: 'Other nations and people of other faiths, apparently were expected to fall into line.'

But the impact of Malvern is evidenced, to a fair degree, in the way it shaped the thinking behind the welfare state. At Oxford, William Temple and R. H. Tawney – who as well as being a key figure from the Christian

Social Union (CSU) went on to become a formative influence in the Labour Party – formed a lasting bond of friendship with William Beveridge. All three were at Balliol College and studied humanities. Beveridge, later a civil servant and educationalist, produced the *Beveridge* Report (officially entitled *Social Insurance and Allied Services*). This became something of a landmark publication, issued in November 1942, and was influential in the framework of the welfare system in post-war Britain. The relationships involved can be seen in the fact that Tawney married Beveridge's sister, Jeanette, and Temple officiated at Beveridge's own marriage. However, after Temple's death in 1944, ICF did not appear to have the same access to those who could influence policy-makers.

Another clear element in ICF's work was its ability to communicate its ideas to ordinary people through its network of directors and missioners. While we can observe its impact on policy-makers, what is much harder to measure is the degree to which the Fellowship was or was not responsible for the shift in public opinion that led to a significant electoral victory for Labour in 1945. This, as much as the aspirations of Beveridge and his colleagues, accounts for the changes that were introduced. But what is clear is that ICF did not enjoy, in its own right, the prominence and influence it had envisaged. One missioner spoke in 1947 about the contrast then with the atmosphere in 1922, when he joined, which he described as one of hope. Now there seemed to be a feeling of uncertainty. Nonetheless, as this chapter shows, ICF was able to find a way forward in the post-war years. The period from 1945 to 1963 is covered here.

Rethinking the role
As it rethought its role, one of ICF's early challenges was the position taken in 1945 by the Church of England Archbishops' report on evangelism, *Towards the Conversion of England*, produced by a group under the chairmanship of the Evangelical Bishop of Rochester, Christopher Chavasse. This stated that the aforementioned national conversion could not be attempted apart from the Anglican parish system, standing in stark contrast to the early convictions of ICF which called for a radical rethink. It also suggested that many within the Church needed to be converted, to come to 'personal knowledge of Christ'. There were elements of the report that ICF affirmed. The Fellowship believed, as Temple had put it, that the Christian message was not being addressed to a nation (Britain) hearing it for the first time but to one that had once accepted it but had now largely forgotten or rejected it. However, ICF was concerned that there seemed to

be a trend to narrow the scope of evangelism, which in turn undermined its own vision of social and moral transformation. It seems that the missions being promoted by more and more Evangelicals, often attaching 'crusade', a term that ICF had originally employed, to their endeavours, were solely about individual conversions.

ICF also explored in the 1940s the possibility of a role in which it co-operated more fully with the Free Churches. A. L. Evan Hopkins, Vicar of Holy Trinity, Folkestone, argued strongly for this at an ICF conference in 1948. Hopkins came from a family which had been involved with the large, interdenominational Keswick Convention, where such co-operation was normal. The chairman, Douglas Crick, Bishop of Chester, had (prior to parish ministry and then his episcopal role) been with the Mersey Mission to Seamen, an interdenominational mission whose object was 'to promote and minister to the spiritual, moral and temporal welfare of Merchant Seamen'. The natural vehicle in which wider ecclesial co-operation could take place was the British Council of Churches, which had been formed in 1942, but the ICF leadership felt that for working together to be effective there needed to be a clearer understanding of the 'line of thought of the ICF'.

In order to achieve this, the Fellowship continued its pre-war approach of encouraging those with different perspectives to talk and listen to one another. In 1950, for example, speakers at its events included trade union leaders, politicians, theologians and parish priests. One trade union speaker was Thomas Williamson (later Sir Thomas Williamson), who was General Secretary of the National Union of General and Municipal Workers (NUGMW) from 1946 to 1961 and was also President of the Trades Union Congress (TUC) in 1957/58. Another speaker was David Gammans (also later knighted), a Conservative MP. He spoke on 'The Christian in Politics'. Charles Raven, who was about to retire as Regius Professor of Divinity at Cambridge University, spoke on the subject of 'Religion and Science', an area in which he was a leading thinker. There was also a presentation on the situation in the parish of Holy Cross, Greenford, which in 1950 was serving 30,000 people, but those linked to the Church were an insignificant number. For ICF, this example underlined the need to meet people in their places of work, and through that to try to set up small Christian 'cells'.

Although ICF had lost none of its clarity of vision, it found itself somewhat struggling to defend its core belief in 'fellowship' – that these various elements belonged in an integrated and interdependent whole. Malvern may have played a vital role in the formation of the welfare state, but this was increasingly perceived in popular thought as having political rather than Christian roots. In its engagement with the Council of Churches, ICF had rightly recognised the importance of a clear understanding of its own identity and purpose if it were not to simply become dissolved into a larger organisation with no real impact. In seeking to better articulate that purpose, it may also have retreated into a more theoretical arena. Although its lectures and publications remained deeply relevant and far-reaching, their impact beyond its own membership is less obvious. While they were able to harness the insights of significant individuals from their fields, those who participated increasingly did so in an individual capacity rather than as a representative of their organisation. They were certainly able to helpfully inform Christian thought, but what became increasingly absent was any sense that these were intended to foster that original vision of a mutual reshaping of society that ICF had been so keen to articulate. Rather than determining the framework of Christian values that should define industrial and economic activities, what might be called a 'Christendom model', the (perhaps unintended) drift was towards encouraging Christians to think and behave in a Christian way within the workplace. To live faithfully in structures defined and operated by others.

To some degree, this could be seen as a sign of the times. While the welfare state had the potential to achieve many of ICF's aspirations in relation to social justice, it relied on an altogether different philosophy – one that largely remains to this day. Rather than seeking a pathway of economic and industrial expansion that, in and of itself, was an expression of common humanity, this was perceived to rely on a 'rebalancing' and redistribution, provided through fiscal and legislative intervention, of the wealth generated by an economic system that policy-makers seemed resigned to assume could not otherwise achieve this end.

It was becoming clear to some that ICF needed to significantly adapt to these emerging realities, which brings again into focus the impact of one of its founding personalities. In 1951, Geoffrey Fisher, who succeeded Temple as Archbishop of Canterbury, was involved in discussions that sought to address this. W. G. Peck, who had now been with ICF for 15 years, told Fisher that for a variety of reasons, one of which was finance, action would need to be taken if ICF were to survive. There were administrative and financial difficulties at the headquarters and at the training centre at Thedden Grange, Hampshire. There had been various attempts to forge a special relationship with the Church Assembly, but they had never worked. Fisher was also briefed by Douglas Crick, who was the current Chair of ICF. Crick was far more outspoken in his critique. He told Fisher that P. T.

R. Kirk, who was still Director, was 'failing', that Kirk's thinking was 'out of date' and that he needed to go. Kirk was then in his seventies. Of the training centre, Crick said that to make this viable twenty students were needed but there were only seven or eight. Crick had doubts about the future of the missioner system. In his view, the Fellowship should have three main functions: to train clergy and ministers who want to be well informed on industrial matters; to have a panel of speakers to participate in events run by management and trade unions; and to be involved in training lay readers and preachers. This was a much less ambitious agenda than the one around which it had been formed, but represented the realities both of the organisation itself and the political and social environment in which it now found itself. It is easy to understand why Kirk would have struggled to embrace this, and in his defence it was only a few years earlier that ICF had anticipated the end of the war, with influential supporters and members in positions of sufficient power and influence to make its Malvern vision a reality.

The issue of training was partly resolved in 1952 when this became for a time located in the Anglican College of the Ascension, which was within the Selly Oak group of colleges in Birmingham. ICF later took over St Brigid's House, another Anglican centre in Selly Oak. The warden of the house was T. Boyard Webster. The number of lay missioners was decreasing but ICF was broadening the scope of the college's work. It now offered courses for a variety of lay people. This included training specifically for lay readers but also courses that sought to help those who were in industrial life to relate their faith to their work. Lecturers were drawn from Birmingham and further afield. There was training for foremen, charge hands and apprentices. One telling reflection of the shifting context was a statement from ICF in 1953 that the most difficult of all problems which the Church had to solve was how it could 'penetrate the invisible screens of custom, outlook and prejudices' which separated industrial life from the spiritual order. In its training it wanted to equip Christians to witness about the reality of 'individual salvation' but also to be able to say something 'about the social and industrial environment in which the new life has to be lived'. It was an error to think 'that the dominion of Christ is limited'.

Mission in different terms
An ongoing debate in the contemporary church is a perceived tension between the role of the pastor-teacher and that of the evangelist. Ministry formation, at least in the eyes of its critics, appears often to be caught in

a tension between the two. In parish terms, it might be argued that ICF's original network of messengers and crusades assumed these two to be distinct, appointing its own representatives to work alongside clergy in reaching people and communities that traditional church structures had failed to engage. As the Fellowship's ongoing story is traced, the reality emerges that the relationship between the two is more complex and interdependent. In reality, an effective pastor-teacher, able to build a rooted and effective community of disciples, can have a significant missional impact; equally those gifted at evangelism will sooner or later need to attend to the pastoral needs of those they engage. As ICF's work moved forward, we can detect a shift towards equipping existing clergy to engage in issues of public life, providing resources to support and inform the people to whom they ministered. But there is an organisational as well as a spiritual dimension to this reality, and the Fellowship too needed to balance its own internal and institutional needs with maintaining its outward vision and impact.

In 1954, Stanley Linsley became General Director. Like Kirk, he was an Anglican clergyman. Before ordination he had worked in engineering, and when he became an Anglican parish minister William Temple encouraged him to take on challenging ministries that included housing estates and a mining area. From the 1930s onwards, Linsley was an ICF supporter. He was Vicar of St Katharine Cree in the City of London, which was the Guild Church for Finance, Commerce and Industry. Under Linsley's leadership, a leaflet was produced called *The Message of the ICF in the Post-War Times*. This began by stating that 'throughout the period between the two world wars, poverty still stalked the land, elementary human rights were left unredressed, and the responsibilities that wealth carried with it were too often ignored.' The narrative did not hesitate to recall that 'the ICF stood out, and proclaimed in Church and street the message of Christ, the friend and Saviour of the poor.' However, with the coming of the welfare state, ICF acknowledged that it had a new challenge, which was 'to conceive its mission in different terms from those of a generation ago, and to fight a battle, in Christ's name, not so much against poverty and social injustice, as against the forces which threaten to enslave the spirit of man *[sic]*.' The concern specifically in mind was an increasingly materialistic and self-seeking society which was emerging particularly in urban centres. It was no longer inevitable that to be part of a major industrial workforce resulted in an inescapable life of poverty and social disadvantage, but those who benefited from more realistic wages and the added benefits of a welfare system did not on the whole respond with grateful Christian allegiance but an increasing attachment to the wealth and personal freedom that they were gradually accumulating.

It was crucial for ICF to address issues that were now current. The campaigns for social justice would certainly continue but some of what the Fellowship, with others, had sought to achieve was coming to fruition. There were hard questions to be asked about the future. ICF was aware of a variety of new enterprises in this period, such as the Iona Community, diocesan missions, Free Church missions and the Worker's Christian Fellowship, and revealed something of its own sense of insecurity by unhelpfully referring to these as 'competition'. There were leaders in the Church of England who strongly supported the contribution made by ICF to the Church, but in 1955 Archbishop Fisher made it clear in conversation that he had not been impressed by what he saw as the 'pink' political colour of the Fellowship, the 'highbrow' note it had struck at times, and some of what he called the 'rantings' of Kirk in the Church Assembly. Under Linsley, Fisher expected change. In this context, ICF developed the theme of the 'wholeness of the gospel', echoing the 'Lord of all life' message that had undergirded much of its training programme, coupled with a message of contemporary human liberation.

It was comparatively easy for Linsley to build new relationships with the Church of England, but we might reflect on the degree to which this was achieved by a tempering of ICF's message. The changed relationship is seen in the fact that, in 1957, Fisher asked ICF's research and training committee to undertake a study of the issue of the social and moral problems of automation. Linsley also saw the need to form partnerships with the Church of England's Industrial Missions, which were beginning to take shape under the leadership of ordained ministers. Ted Wickham was a pioneer in this area. He began his industrial chaplaincy work in a munitions factory in the Potteries (in Staffordshire) and then moved to Sheffield, where he had a significant impact. In view of Wickham's ministry, ICF withdrew their own local missioner. Wickham was to argue for the important role of ICF in offering a broader perspective on which chaplaincy could draw. In 1958, with the number of missioners continuing to decline, the Fellowship began to allocate finance to local clergy engaged in industrial chaplaincy. By this time the system of Area Directors who had been responsible for missioners was coming to an end, although it still operated through contacts in the various regions of the country.

Mission was not disappearing from the ICF agenda in this period. The language of 'crusade' was used by Billy Graham during his meetings in the Harringay Arena, London, in 1954, which attracted an aggregate attendance of over two million. ICF's traditional crusades were still happening, but on a much smaller scale. The emphasis came to be placed on longer-term mission in a locality, in which parishes were fully involved, and on commitment to ongoing change. ICF wanted to provide training and literature to assist those in the parishes who were involved in mission that took the context of work seriously. One missioner commented in 1957 on some church people being 'timid' or 'dumbfounded' when it came to witnessing. As regards the ICF message itself, there was a call for a 'sound theology' for contextual mission, and for theologians who could write well. Reference was made to B. F. Westcott, Charles Gore and Henry Scott Holland, the formative thinkers of the CSU. In the 1950s, no major thinker associated closely with ICF emerged. However, clergy training days, study groups and visits to schools, which had been adversely affected by the war, were revived.

There was a recognition even in the 1950s that wider society in Britain was gradually becoming more distant from Christian faith. Easter, which had traditionally been a time when churches could expect the Christian message to be covered in the press, was increasingly regarded simply as a holiday period. It was also recognised that new methods of communication were needed. ICF used a film strip, at the time an emerging and innovative medium, which had been produced by SPCK on 'The Gospel and Modern Society'. It convened discussion groups to address such topics as home, family, neighbourhood and community in a time of changing social patterns. The best way to undertake mission in the expanding new housing areas was another topic. Well-known speakers took up various subjects at some of the ICF Council meetings, which from 1956 were chaired by Stretton Reeve, Bishop of Lichfield. One speaker was George Woodcock, the Assistant General Secretary (and later General Secretary) of the TUC, who was a committed Roman Catholic. His theme was the purpose of work. The Council also talked about ongoing financial needs. Regular income was falling, although legacies helped to offset the decline. We can begin to detect how through this period the differing personalities of those who succeeded Kirk influenced the various directions that the Fellowship took. Linsley was effective in strengthening ties with the Church of England and securing the ongoing endorsement of its senior figures. He was realistic about its financial limitations and it would also seem that he was able to recognise what was necessary to move forward. What he appeared less able to do was inspire others with ICF's enduring vision or secure the services of individuals who could fulfil this role. In 1958, Stanley Linsley became Vicar and Rural Dean of Kidderminster and it was clear that someone who could attract greater support for the work of the Fellowship needed to succeed him.

Fresh leadership

The person the Executive approached was Stephan Hopkinson. He had studied at Wadham College, Oxford, and then went to Mexico to work for an oil company. During this time, he felt a call to Anglican ministry. He had been greatly influenced by Archbishop William Temple's teaching on the need for the Church to be concerned with social and political issues. Hopkinson trained at Lincoln Theological College, where a further influence was Michael Ramsey, a future Archbishop of Canterbury, who was a college tutor. During the war Hopkinson was Vicar of St John's Church in the shipbuilding town of Barrow-in-Furness and in 1943 he became Vicar of the large parish of Battersea. He was unimpressed by the church's ornate windows, and claimed that after one heavy air raid he decided to take matters into his own hands and he smashed 'the Victorian glass'. Within his actions and temperament, we might detect something of the same spirit as ICF's legendary messenger Geoffrey Studdert Kennedy who once famously declared: 'If finding God in our churches leads to us losing Him in our factories, then better we tear down those churches for God must hate the sight of them.'

In 1952, Hopkinson was appointed Vicar of St Mary Woolnoth in the City of London. He was also a Navy Chaplain. When Hopkinson accepted the invitation to become General Director, he moved from one City church, St Mary Woolnoth, to another, St Katharine Cree, on the north side of Leadenhall Street. This was to provide a headquarters for the Fellowship.

ICF was presented with significant opportunities at this point. It had secured the services of Hopkinson, then aged fifty, who had wide experience, and while he may not have had the public profile of Studdert Kennedy, he was an outstanding communicator and was known for his enormous energy. A second opportunity was the offer of St Katharine Cree as a headquarters. It was in a poor state of repair but ICF agreed to restore it and add several offices for staff. Financial help from the Diocese of London was promised, and the Diocese also made a commitment to pay two-thirds of Hopkinson's salary. Another development was that a substantial house connected with St George's Church, Wolverhampton (and later another house in Burton-on-Trent) became available for its use. This was to contribute to a sense of communal identity. Finally, a group of Fleet Street journalists who were involved in a Christian newspaper, *The Leader*, which had a circulation of about 30,000 copies, reached an agreement whereby ICF paid the newspaper each month for material which it supplied to be included.

As he talked to others, Hopkinson saw that some of the traditional functions carried out by ICF were no longer relevant. With some regret, recruitment of lay missioners came to an end. During his time in office, Hopkinson became Anglican Adviser to Associated Television, which at the time had a considerable output of religious programmes. Although the role was advisory, he became an effective producer and presenter of programmes. Hopkinson was also keen that ICF should be popular in style. By 1960, there were more than 200 new pamphlets and booklets. Hopkinson's own books included *God at Work: The Working World and the Kingdom of God* (Hodder & Stoughton, 1962) and *Creator Spirit* (SPCK, 1963).

Spirituality and mission

In many ways, Hopkinson was able to embody much of what ICF had sought to become in the early years after its formation. His desire was for it to be outward-looking, and for it to avoid the trap of the organised churches which he described as allocating 95 per cent of their effort to 5 per cent of the population. But he also recognised the need for inward renewal. As he travelled and met the various groups of members, he stressed the place of fellowship. Despite the ending of recruitment of new missioners, a handful remained, and there were still over 40 local ICF groups, or 'branches' (a name that was being used less frequently), across the country. The change of name reflects the fact that many had developed a degree of local identity. Some, such as those in Manchester, Wolverhampton, Birmingham, Tynemouth, Stoke-on-Trent, Burton-on-Trent, Bristol, Brighton and North and South Wales, held a variety of events and, with the demise of Area Directors, they now related directly with the office at St Katherine Cree, with which they were regularly in touch. The activities they arranged depended in part on local secretaries who acted as key points of contact. Hopkinson commended the view that men and women of 'prayer and action' were to be seen as 'the strongest people in the world, for this is the only unbreakable combination'. The aim was to build up an articulate, thoughtful and prayerful membership that would support Christians in industry. The language and activity that was now in common use reflected an organisation that was less about deployment, with 'missioners' and 'messengers' embarking on 'crusades', and more a network of local activists drawn together around a shared vision. The degree to which this was the outcome of a change of leadership, a reflection of more general trends in society or the inevitable evolution of an organisation is hard to tell. Probably all three were influences, but this had the potential to serve ICF's cause well in the new environment in which it found itself.

Another indicator of how local groups were developing is the new step taken in 1959 to form a 'Brotherhood'. Initially the focus was on ICF work being done in the Midlands, particularly in Birmingham and Wolverhampton. The full name was the Brotherhood of Prayer and Action in Association with the Industrial Christian Fellowship. Prayers of St Francis of Assisi, which emphasised God at work in all things ('The Canticle of the Creatures') and being God's instruments ('Make me a Channel of your Peace') were central to its thinking. The Brotherhood was a largely 'dispersed community' living by a Rule of Life. A core community lived in St George's House in Wolverhampton. Its full members were lay people and the initial cohort were listed by name and also by occupation. They included a fitter, a labourer, a fitter and mechanic, an aircraft fitter, a slater, a student, a schoolteacher, a parish worker, an ICF missioner and a physiotherapist. There were three clergy associated with it. Six women were associates: they were wives of full members.

Revised 'objects', or objectives, for ICF were also drafted in 1959. Slightly different wording appeared in different documents. The main features had been fairly constant since the 1920s and were retained, but there were new emphases, which perhaps also reflected the emerging activities at grassroots level. First, they outlined the belief that it was called to 'witness in the power of the Spirit to the Fatherhood of God, the Brotherhood in Christ of all mankind – whatever their race or calling – and the advent of the Kingdom of God'. We might detect the influence of the 'Brotherhood' here, but the more inclusive idea of any 'race or calling' was also significant in the context of race relations issues in Britain. However, the terminology used would indicate that ICF, visionary in so many other areas, still had much to consider in relation to the inclusion of women. The second aim was to 'minister to all engaged in the work of the world, seeking to win them to discipleship, to Jesus Christ as the Redeemer of mankind and the Lord of all life, and to unite them in fellowship and prayer as living members of the Body of Christ's Church'. The previous wording had spoken of bringing people into 'a bond of Christian fellowship and prayer'. The new wording also emphasised life in the Church. Thirdly, there was a desire to encourage 'study under the guidance of the Holy Spirit', to discover more about 'how to apply the truths of Christianity to the social, economic and industrial situation of our time and to take such action as may seem good'.

It is clear that there was a vision in the late 1950s and early 1960s of ICF contributing to deeper engagement with issues regarding living a spiritual life in the world. Whereas in its early days, it was seeking to establish an internationally recognised political and economic order in which the values of God's Kingdom were embedded within its very structures, its emphasis seemed quite clearly to have become one where those Christian values were exemplified by those who acted as intentional disciples of Jesus within those structures. David Wood, the Vicar of St George's Church, Wolverhampton (with which St George's House was linked), affirmed in 1960 his belief that 'in the will of God' the Brotherhood could play a part in giving new life to ICF. Wood and others who were involved in the shaping of the Brotherhood were seeking – as they put it – to find a balance between 'the sacramental discipline and the evangelical witness of the Anglican tradition'. Beyond this there was the hope of involving Christians from other traditions. All those who were committed to the Brotherhood followed a pattern of morning prayer, midday prayer if that was possible within the workplace, and evening prayer, which was compline or something similar. Those who could get to the headquarters in London or to St George's House, Wolverhampton, had Holy Communion together at 6.30 a.m. and then a 'fellowship breakfast'.

The first national conference of the Brotherhood was held in April 1961. It was led by David Wood. By this time, there were more members than a year before. It was agreed that supplementary training for Anglican ordinands, to enable them to gain insights into industrial life, would be offered at St George's House. The training that had been available at St Brigid's House had come to an end. There were still nine serving lay missioners at this stage, and under the influence of the Brotherhood four were living in communal houses. However, the precise relationship between ICF and the Brotherhood was unclear. Hopkinson and Wood did not achieve a close working relationship, partly because both were travelling a great deal. This included international engagements. In 1962, Wood visited South Africa and Northern Rhodesia. He met Anglican bishops who expressed their disappointment about the lack of support from England in their struggles against oppression. Hopkinson, in the meantime, was in the USA. At the end of 1962, Wood resigned as Vicar of St George's, having served for seven years. The two organisations increasingly went their separate ways, with the Brotherhood placing its emphasis on monastic-type communities, such as one in Cable Street, east London, which had a ministry to homeless men.

Wider movements

One of the wider movements that had a major impact on the work of ICF was Industrial Mission. In 1959, the Industrial Mission Association was formed with the intention of ensuring the ongoing development of this ministry, especially in connection with the work of industrial chaplains. Ted Wickham, one of those at the forefront of the movement when he was in Sheffield, became Bishop of Middleton, in the Diocese of Manchester, in the same year, remaining until his retirement. While doing all he could to encourage industrial mission undertaken under the auspices of the Church of England, he was also committed to ecumenism. His published works include *Church and People in an Industrial City* (1964), which drew from his Sheffield experiences. Another important figure in this field was Colin Cuttell. He was the first clergyman to be a full-time industrial missioner in London. The South London Industrial Mission (SLIM) was formed in 1956. Cuttell was supported by Cuthbert Bardsley, Bishop of Croydon, who had been influenced by Studdert Kennedy. Cuttell was able to engage with employers, managers, trade union leaders and workers in the factories.

By 1963, ICF was involved in partnership connections with new initiatives in industrial mission in various parts of the country. In some instances, these were established by Anglican dioceses, with – as in south London – some of the bishops taking an active interest. In other cases, it developed from the grassroots. In east London, for example, John Groser, an Anglican priest, built up a centre which included Worker's Educational Association courses, with which ICF had long-standing links; a yearly course for newly ordained clergy on 'The Task of the Church in Industrial Society'; and specific seminars, for example on 'The Church and the Trade Union Movement'. A wider Metropolitan Industrial Mission was formed, with representatives from dioceses such as London, Southwark, Chelmsford and Rochester.

The number of industrial chaplains across the country grew by the 1960s to over a hundred, both part time and full time. As well as working on the front line, some were committed to research, and the Fellowship was keen to be involved in this. It also wanted to bring together Church of England, Free Church and Roman Catholic chaplains – not only those in industry but also others, such as prison chaplains – and to discuss issues, including theological perspectives, with a view to implementing findings that emerged. Again, we can detect how the foundational ideas of ICF were valued and through partnership enabled to take root in an emerging organisation. It had lost none of its critical edge, evidenced by an occasion when an ICF member warned of the danger of forgetting theology and ending up with 'industrianity' in place of Christianity.

Hopkinson attempted to take full advantage of the opportunities which he saw available. He travelled widely, speaking at events and connecting with individuals. Some of his work was behind the scenes, bringing management and trade union representatives together. In 1961, Hopkinson became part of a group of 18 leaders from churches and from industry which met several times between then and 1963. The meetings were mainly held in Marlow, Buckinghamshire, and out of this came the Marlow Declaration on the Church and industry. The research was funded by bodies interested in education. The Declaration offered perspectives regarding styles of leadership, training, work–life balance and safety issues in industrial and social life. It was widely distributed, with at least 75,000 copies in circulation, and the text was sometimes accompanied by commentary. An ICF address based on its outcomes was delivered in 1963. The Catholic Social Guild produced a commentary by Michael Patrick Fogarty, a Liberal politician and academic. Several companies reproduced it in their house magazines. The Declaration was seen by ICF as helping to create fresh attitudes of mind in a world increasingly committed to dictatorship, materialism and self-interest. The theme of co-operation in industry, something dependent on mutual trust, had been a long-standing ICF theme which Hopkinson was glad to see included. However, he accepted that there was a certain 'pedestrian quality' in much of the wording. There was nothing to disagree with, but would it make a difference?

Counting the cost

These promising steps forward revealed both the ongoing potential of ICF and the inheritance it carried, but there were also significant setbacks. The budgeted £20,000 maximum cost for the redevelopment St Katharine Cree became £46,000. Members of the Executive either did not see the figures or did not realise the gravity of the situation. In this period, it comprised 12 clergy and 14 lay members, although it had now achieved an improved gender balance with half of these being women. Charles Claxton, Bishop of Blackburn, who had taken over from Douglas Crick as Chairman, expressed his 'horror and dismay' when this massive overspend came to light. One comment made was that Hopkinson had a gift of 'spinning words', with the clear implication that at times he did not communicate unpalatable realities.

In many respects, this illustrates the challenge that ICF faced as an organisation that had lost nothing of its vision but was seeking to operate with significantly reduced resources. In its formative years, Kirk had been able to focus intently on its organisational infrastructure, while employing individuals like Studdert Kennedy and other charismatic missioners to be its outward face. Now both roles seemed expected of its director. Linsley had certainly been attentive to his organisational responsibilities but at the expense of its public impact, whereas Hopkinson had regained that wider impact but had neglected its internal operations. ICF would not be the only organisation to have appointed a prophetic and dynamic figure in a key moment of crisis, only to then encumber them with administrative duties or to suffer the consequences of these being overlooked.

Another disappointment was that *The Leader* had ceased publication after a relatively short life. The expenditure on St Katharine Cree meant that to avoid the organisation closing altogether – the situation was described by one commentator as 'near bankruptcy' – the number of office staff had to be reduced. In 1963, Hopkinson resigned from his position and became the Bishop of Chelmsford's industrial adviser. He continued his work in broadcasting, which included arranging services to be broadcast from local churches, and took on a parish in Essex.

The picture in 1963 was a mixed one. On the one hand, the ICF message about faith and work was spreading. There were by then similar organisations in several countries and it was known that Industrial Sunday was observed in Canada, Australia, New Zealand, South Africa, British Guiana, the West Indies, Germany, Japan and the USA. From the 1960s, some congregations combined Industrial Sunday with Rogation Sunday, the day when churches traditionally offered prayer for God's blessing on the fruits of the earth and those producing food. But there was a recognition that, in what was becoming a post-industrial society, ICF needed to revisit its aims. The Fellowship now stated that it aimed to apply the Christian faith to daily work in fair dealing, good relationships and good workmanship, and to build up, with industrial chaplains, a body of men and women pledged to make a Christian impact where they lived and worked. It observed that at one time it was the only body committed to mission in the industrial context, but was happy to recognise that this was no longer the case and to celebrate the number of experiments in industrial mission across the country and the world. The role of ICF into the future was to support Industrial Mission, maintain St Katharine Cree as a centre for study, foster a fellowship of Christians concerned about industrial issues, and support Industrial Sunday.

When Stephan Hopkinson announced in 1963 that he was moving on, Claxton described himself as 'deeply concerned' about finding the right successor. He was fully aware of the organisation's history. Three years previously the Fellowship had celebrated 40 years since the Navvy Mission Society and the Christian Social Union had united to create it. Claxton believed that the need was for someone who could look into what might be its task in the coming decades. In setting this out for the Executive, he wrote: 'We shall need someone who could do some solid thinking and research into some of our industrial problems and try to gather at St Katharine Cree a group of people who can share in this with him.' The future was to contain advances but also difficulties. Perhaps as a visual representation of that, a series of drawings was featured in 1963 in St Katharine Cree depicting the Stations of the Cross. They were painted by a Romanian, Arnold Daghani, who had spent time in a prison camp and had escaped. His message was of hope in the midst of suffering. The person who arrived to take on the leadership of ICF was Charles Branch, who brought with him the experience of being an industrial chaplain.

As we end this chapter in 1963 we can reflect that this was the year of the publication of John Robinson's *Honest to God*. The book suggested that people of the time had rejected the concept of God 'up there' but needed to recognise that the idea of God who was 'out there' in the world of life and work was also a simplification of theology. The latter would be perceived by many as being central to the vision of ICF, as indeed it was in the Navvy Mission before. Robinson suggested that the Church should instead reflect on a concept of God, proposed by the theologian Paul Tillich, as 'the ground of our being'. This suggests that a secular world requires a secular theology, where God's continuing revelation comes through the whole of human experience and not only through religion and Church. He also introduced the understanding of situational ethics where moral codes can be subject to circumstances. These are realities that prevail to the current day.

His views were controversial, and the book was almost universally condemned by traditionalists, but was hailed as a breath of fresh air by many liberals. Michael Ramsey, Archbishop of Canterbury, was less enthusiastic. In its desire to relate faith for the working community, the views of *Honest to*

God are a word of warning for the role of ICF going forward. Being relevant to the society and working situations is important, but not at the expense of losing sight of God who wishes to transform human lives and through those transformed lives to transform other individuals, the workplace and society as a whole.

Chapter 6

A small Fellowship
with a rich vision

At a riverbank in Babylon, a group of music makers and priests sat in bewilderment as they viewed a landscape that was unrecognisable and seemed to contradict everything they knew. Their despair and confusion are recorded in the words of Psalm 137 as they discarded the tools of their trade, heard the taunts of their opponents ringing in their ears, but determined that they would never give up on the world they had been wrenched from. They knew what it was to live in a society that was founded and organised according to the purposes of God, though the tirades of earlier prophets suggest that this might have been more rhetoric than reality. But their land had been invaded, their sacred city left in tatters, and they were being forcibly removed into exile. The crisis that their Psalm of lament succinctly captures is one that many scholars of Old Testament history recognise as a key watershed. Their question, 'How do we sing the Lord's song in a strange land?', was answered through literature and a mindset of 'diaspora' – expressing an identity as God's people not through the building of a state which exemplified this but living faithfully, and at times subversively, within the power structures of others. But the Psalm writers could not take their eyes off Jerusalem, and a final stanza which is all too often avoided in contemporary exposition, refuses to encounter this new reality and instead can only offer resentment and brutal retribution.

The term 'new Jerusalem' has often been attached to the vision for British society that emerged from both world wars, and as we look back over the previous chapter, Kirk might well be described as one whose eyes remained fixed on that goal. But it was a vision that increasingly eluded him. Perhaps, if given the chance, he might draw comfort from recognising in the oracles of those Old Testament prophets that, even when such a Jerusalem did exist, it proved itself all too capable of becoming a state that can 'trample on the heads of the poor as on the dust of the ground and deny justice to the oppressed.'

The years that followed Kirk's leadership might be described as a period in which The Industrial Christian Fellowship (ICF) sought to negotiate its place in this increasingly 'strange land'. Like the Psalm writers of Babylon, it did not easily release its belief that a new Jerusalem could be established, but it was also finding itself increasingly exiled from the seats of power and influence where such ideals might be pursued. Yet the 1960s were the decade that made clear that any future for ICF relied on helping people live out its vision in a world that it could only seriously influence through their convictions, and less so as an end in itself. Church and State alike were not unwilling to hear and genuinely value its insights, but each had their own place in the emerging landscape and ICF would need to find its own way of residing there too.

In 1964, this new era was embraced with Stephan Hopkinson moving on from the role of director. The subsequent years have been seen more widely as a period in which Britain began to lose the sense of being shaped by a Christian framework of belief. Within the Christian community, divergent forces were at work. While the Church of England continued to enjoy some degree of preferential influence, organised Christianity was taking on a far more ecumenical flavour. The publication of *Honest to God* raised important questions about traditional understandings of God. Some subsequent trends in theology were addressed by ICF: for example, Helena Charles, in 1965, analysed the work of some theological authors and affirmed the orthodoxy which had characterised the Christian Social Union. This was also the period when the charismatic movement, with its sense of the immediacy of the work of the Holy Spirit, began to grow. These different elements in the wider social and spiritual environment had a relatively limited impact on ICF, which continued to focus on issues relating to the world of work. This chapter traces its development from 1964 to 1990.

Promoting perspectives on faith at work
The appointment of Charles Branch as Director was intended to bring his first-hand experience of being Vicar of Holy Trinity, Ipswich, and his wide involvement in industrial chaplaincy to bear on the Fellowship. The change of role, to a national one, seems not to have suited Branch, who remained only two years in the post. However, he did oversee the

launch of an important publication, the *ICF Quarterly*, which proved to be influential. Branch hoped that ICF could develop more ecumenical links – with the British Council of Churches and also with Roman Catholics who were working at the interface of the Church and industry. But after Branch resigned, the Fellowship looked once again to an Anglican figure for leadership and appointed Nicholas Brown, who from 1967 combined the director's role with being part-time Secretary of the Industrial Committee of the Board for Social Responsibility of the Church of England. He was to continue this work for a decade.

Brown brought to ICF strategic thinking about its contribution to an understanding of faith at work and also energetic implementation of decisions that were made. Publishing activities now came under ICF Press Ltd, which as well as printing the *ICF Quarterly* also produced a larger (though short-lived) publication called *Compass*, and printed (free of charge) the *Industrial Mission* journal. Lectures and exhibitions were started in St Katharine Cree, and during the later 1960s there was a pattern of conferences taking place across the country. As an example, ICF co-sponsored a conference in Blackpool, on the topic 'Church and Industry'. Academics, managers, trade union representatives and some members of what had been the Christendom group attended. The Christendom group, which for many years had held summer schools in Oxford, had now thrown in its lot with ICF. Although Anglicans were still by far the largest denominational group at these conferences, Roman Catholics and members of Free Churches also attended.

There were now no ICF personnel involved in larger-scale missions. Norman Barnes was employed to do some deputation work, but this was undertaken largely in connection with churches and various Christian groups. A full-time Assistant Secretary, David Wardrop, was appointed to strengthen the central operation. He had been the Bishop of Exeter's Chaplain for ecumenical relations. For outward-directed witness, ICF's emphasis had changed to supporting local industrial mission, and the policy of giving partial financial support to Anglican priests involved in industrial mission was further developed. In 1967, ten were receiving support. Overseas missioners were also occasionally sponsored, such as an African Anglican priest, Jacob Rasmenni. He was a student at the William Temple College in Rugby, which offered training for those wanting to undertake effective ministry in the secular world. Rasmenni went on to become an Industrial Chaplain in Africa. The Principal of the William Temple College was Mollie Batten, who had studied theology at St Anne's

College, Oxford. She gave the Fellowship considerable support. Her vision was of bringing together people from industry, social work and education.

In the period 1967 to 1969, a series of teach-ins was organised at St Katharine Cree and other locations around the country, on such subjects as 'Patterns of Employment' and 'Technology and Innovation'. The headquarters also hosted well-attended lunchtime talks, with speakers such as Alastair Burnet of *The Economist* and Baroness Mary Stocks, an educationalist. In 1967, an ICF-linked service was arranged at St Paul's Cathedral. This type of service was later repeated. The preacher at St Paul's in 1967 was Geoffrey Lampe, who was Ely (later Regius) Professor of Divinity at Cambridge University. He preached a sermon on 'God in a Monday world'. The idea of 'God on Monday' was to become a popular one. In the following year, ICF organised a major event in Plymouth, to look at workplace issues in the region. Those participating included business people, academics, workers' representatives and managers. Political questions were also discussed. David Owen MP, who was to become Foreign Secretary, was one of the speakers. One questioner, from Cornwall, said that a great deal was heard about Britain joining the Common Market (Owen was a strong supporter of this move) but wondered when this far-westerly region 'could join Great Britain'. One reaction to this event indicates that, while ICF was having to adapt to prevailing circumstances, it had not lost its core vision, the value and necessity of which could still be recognised. A TV presenter who was there commented: 'No other single organisation but ICF could have succeeded half so well in bringing together people so that they could express their divergent opinions to each other.'

The impact that political views had on race relations and industrial relations contributed to the fact that political issues appeared quite regularly in the *ICF Quarterly* in the later 1960s. Paul Johnson, the historian and journalist, wrote an article in 1968 claiming there might be a need for Labour MPs to act specifically to oppose 'the ugly spirit which is being nourished in Britain'. Johnson spoke of the 'chaotic imaginings' of Enoch Powell. The background was Powell's 'Rivers of Blood' speech of that year, which criticised the rates of immigration into the UK, especially from Commonwealth countries. Johnson argued that this 'ugly spirit' towards others was the real 'enemy within'. There were contributions to the *ICF Quarterly* in 1970 from Anthony Crosland of *The Guardian* and Michael Shanks of *The Times*. Following the election of that year, in which a Conservative Government led by Edward Heath came to power, it published an article by Sir Geoffrey Howe, then Solicitor General, making a case for the Government's Industrial Relations Bill. A reply was published from Jim Conway, General Secretary of the Amalgamated Union of Engineering Workers, in which he stated – and this was common union thinking – that the Conservatives wanted to 'hamstring the unions'. ICF did not, however, want to focus on party politics. It considered that industrial chaplains, of whom there were now about 90, had important insights, and published articles from an Anglican chaplain in Norwich and a Baptist chaplain in South Wales.

Human values and technological change
ICF continued to seek opportunities to initiate and influence public debate and spent three years preparing for a major study conference in 1971 on 'Human Values and Technical Change'. The conference was intended to reflect changes over the 30 years since Malvern in 1941. The venue was St John's College, Cambridge. There were three co-chairs: Sir Robert Birley, Professor of Social Science and the Humanities at City University, London; John Partridge, President of the Confederation of British Industry (CBI); and Victor Feather, General Secretary of the Trades Union Congress (TUC). The conference was, therefore, operating at an influential level. It also had ecumenical breadth, as it was affirmed by the Archbishop of Canterbury, the Cardinal Archbishop of Westminster and the Moderator of the Free Church Federal Council. A great deal was done in the preparatory period by Nicholas Brown, Mollie Batten and Ethel Kirkham, ICF Administrator. Preparatory papers for Cambridge included several theological papers: Geoffrey Lampe on 'Poverty and Affluence: The Traditions of Christian Life and Discipline'; Ninian Smart, who had established the first Department of Religious Studies in Britain, at the University of Lancaster, on 'World Religions and Technical Change'; and Don Cupitt, Lecturer in Philosophy of Religion at Cambridge University, on 'Ethics and Technical Change'.

The conference attracted 180 participants, which was comparable to Malvern. Those identified as from the professions numbered 55, with 44 from industry. Two plenary papers opened the conference. Robert Birley spoke on 'Authority and Power in a Free Society', and Philip Shelbourne, Chief Executive of a merchant bank, spoke on 'Economic and Financial Considerations'. Two other plenary speakers were Richard O'Brien, Deputy Chairman of a division of the Delta Metal Company and also an adviser on industry to the recent Labour Government, and Sir Frederick Seebohm, Chairman of Barclays Bank International. Only ten conference members were from the trade unions; the emphasis was shifting to business. Of the

14 interdisciplinary groups that met during the conference, there was one on trade unions. Mollie Batten led a group on power from a Christian perspective, which included workplace power relationships. Among the other topics were science and technology, behavioural and social sciences, mass media, wages and taxation, and industrial relations. A paper that had been given at Malvern by Dorothy L. Sayers was studied: this addressed the Church's responsibilities in a wide-ranging way. In his summing up at the end of the conference, Nicholas Brown said that what had been done was 'theology'. This was true to an extent, although some of what was presented and discussed contained little that was explicitly Christian.

Within the field of the environment and of environmental consciousness, important moves were made in the 1970s. Indeed, the decade has been known as 'the decade of the environment'. Edward Heath created the Department of the Environment in 1970, with the Secretary of State for the Environment as a cabinet position. Enviromental issues had been previously raised in the 1960s by Rachel Carson, whose book *Silent Spring*, published in 1962, drew attention to the dangers of pesticides such as DDT; and by Lynn White in his work *The Historical Roots of Our Ecologic Crisis*, published in 1967, where he critiqued the Christian view of dominion over creation (Genesis 1:28) being a command of God. ICF was at the forefront of this call for a changed approach to environmental issues, though we might also note that this was a theme it had raised some 30 years earlier in one of the more neglected declarations that emerged from Malvern. The *ICF Quarterly* carried an article in 1970 by C. F. D Moule, Lady Margaret's Professor of Divinity at Cambridge, on the topic of humanity and nature in the New Testament. This had been delivered as a lecture and had attracted considerable attention. Moule's argument was that the Bible portrayed ways in which appropriate interaction with nature could take place, and that 'use or abuse of nature has far-reaching results in the whole structure of the world, inanimate as well as animate'. The *Quarterly* offered a bibliography on topics related to environmental responsibility, conservation and pollution. Nicholas Brown, who took a particular interest in this subject, organised an exhibition on conservation at St Katharine Cree. There was also a recital of 'Conservation Songs', sung by Suzanne Harris, a well-known folk singer, and others. An evening reception was co-hosted by Robert Stopford, Bishop of London, and Sir Charles Trinder, who had been Lord Mayor of London. ICF helped to put conservation on the churches' agenda.

In the follow-up by ICF after the Cambridge Conference, another crucial area given continuing attention was industrial relations. In the context of massive industrial strife in Britain, the possibility of a more co-operative relationship between management and employees was explored. Richard O'Brien wrote on this in the *Quarterly*, having addressed it at Cambridge. The *Quarterly* continued to carry articles offering different perspectives, for example in analysis of the national dock strike of 1970 and the miners' strike of 1972. Trade union views on the 'Dock Struggle' were conveyed and there was an article by Ian Ramsey, Bishop of Durham, on the miners' strike. In the same period, John Partridge, Vice-President of the CBI and Chairman of Imperial Group Ltd, offered thoughts on industrial relations in the European Economic Community (EEC). Commenting on issues raised at the Cambridge Conference, he said that as a 'hardened conferencer' he regarded the conference as 'one of the most valuable contributions to the discussion and analysis of our current social problems in recent years'. In 1973, Denmark, Ireland and the UK joined the EEC, and Michael Shanks, an ICF adviser, who had been a Director of British Leyland, took up a post in that year as Head of the Social Affairs Directorate in Brussels.

It seemed up to 1974 that ICF was maintaining a role at a time of technological change. Among the speakers at ICF dinners were Sir Frank Figgures, Director of the National Economic Development Office, and Len Murray, Assistant General Secretary of the TUC. There were suggestions of renaming ICF as a 'Forum', with conferences and talks now being seen as core activities. The *Quarterly* had a circulation of 18,000 and it was thought there was no other national journal of this kind produced by the churches. However, in 1974, problems became apparent, which might indicate the degree to which ICF remained reliant upon the energy and endeavours of its director. Nicholas Brown was taken ill, and although he continued until 1977, there was talk of merging with some other organisation. Negotiations with the William Temple Association were initiated, with Mollie Batten central to these, but a merger did not happen. Subscription income dropped to one-third of the 1963 level and donations and church collections had halved. Interest on the legacies now accounted for a quarter of all income. Charles Claxton stepped down from his role as chair, and it proved difficult to find a replacement. There was also talk of being absorbed into Industrial Mission, but there was a view in the Church of England that ICF, although now much smaller, had a 'degree of independence' which should be prized.

New prophetic engagement
Hereward Cooke, who had been an Anglican minister in Rugby and whose earlier background was in chartered accountancy, was appointed Director

in 1977, and he was able to bring the Fellowship's finances under control. At this stage, it had 750 members and £40,000 in assets. Kenneth Adams took over from Laurence Brown, Bishop of Birmingham, as Chairman. Adams had been an officer in the Army, then a director of a commercial organisation. He moved to become Director of Studies at St George's House, Windsor Castle, which had been founded in 1966 as a place where people with responsibility in different areas of society could come together to explore contemporary issues. Adams, an Anglican, was also Vice-Chairman of the Archbishops' Council on Evangelism and he had a great interest in industrial mission. He was the first chairman of ICF who was not a senior cleric. Adams considered that the organisation, though now 'small in number', was 'rich in the vision of its purpose'. He also saw a great need for 'prophetic teaching' which contained powerful application to people's activities at work.

For Hereward Cooke and Kenneth Adams, it was important to work together with the Industrial Committee of the General Synod of the Church of England and the British Council of Churches. In 1977, a one-day consultation sponsored by the three bodies was held at Church House on the subject of 'Fairness and Justice'. Eight main speakers brought their own particular perspectives, described as Christian, pragmatic, socialist and humanist. There were common concerns about issues of injustice: the unfair spread of government spending across the country; the lack of respect for individuals shown by bureaucratic machines; the multinationals that were not looking at the concerns of employees; the self-seeking of power groups; and the callous attitude to what was then called the Third World by the world's rich. It is at this conference that we might detect that, for all its effectiveness, ICF was struggling to maintain a clear sense of its distinct identity, at least in the eyes of those outside it. Paul Brett of the Industrial Committee made the observation that it was only duplicating the work of Industrial Mission. In reply, Adams argued that the Fellowship's work was 'entirely complementary to that of Industrial Mission' and that it concentrated on those already Christian. This may have clarified ICF's sense of purpose, but this was in marked contrast to early emphases on evangelism and crusades. This is not to say that its role in seeking to provide for Christians in their workplaces was not previously important but there now existed a conscious shift in focus.

In autumn 1977, an ICF Annual Lecture was started. Typically, about 70 attended, with the venue being St Katharine Cree. The first of these was delivered by Ted Wickham. He considered the Church's contribution to the regeneration of Britain, urging the presentation of 'biblical-Christian faith' in contemporary terms and also urged the Church to 'speak prophetically to the problems and crises of our period of history'. The 1978 lecture was given by Sir Fred Catherwood, Chairman of the British Overseas Trade Board and Director General of the National Economic Development Council. He was the author of the very influential book, *The Christian in Industrial Society*. The topic of his lecture was 'Work as unto God'. He argued that God had made human beings with a creative instinct and this was to be expressed in work. He saw technology in positive terms and pointed to examples around the world of advances in technology being linked with high employment levels rather than such advances putting people out of work. For Catherwood, the moral perspective on work was important, and he was concerned about what he saw as a 'collapse' of the moral foundation of the trade union movement. However, he was convinced that to try to impose the personal morality of Christians by law on a reluctant citizenry did the Christian faith no good.

The *ICF Quarterly* took up a number of themes in the later 1970s. Donald Coggan, as Archbishop of Canterbury, wrote in support of ICF's role as a 'catalytic body'. One issue was on the theme of prayer in relation to work. The articles ranged widely. As well as those by Anglicans, there was one by Michael Hollings, a Roman Catholic, and another by Donald Vallance, a Baptist. There was an emphasis in another issue on thinking about the ways 'industrial and commercial work' could benefit from 'the inspiration of Christian thought and action'. ICF wanted to see work as something offered to God, and its magazine lamented that Industrial Sunday was much less in evidence (though there was some stress on industry on Rogation Sunday) and that work did not feature with any regularity in worship. A critique was also offered in a 1978 edition of the way Industrial Mission was, as Hilda Flint put it, 'entrenched in a man's world'. She was on the Executive Committee of the South London Industrial Mission, and spoke of the 'truly liberating gospel – for men and women', which was available in mission. She called for greater exploration of 'a Kingdom in which masculinity and femininity are fully developed, regardless of the sexist preconceptions which imprison and restrict human relationships'. By this time, women accounted for almost 40 per cent of the British workforce. Just as ICF was speaking of environmental issues more than a decade before they entered mainstream debate, so it similarly became an advocate for issues of gender justice in the workplace at an early stage in the nation's emerging consciousness.

Though again, it might also be accused of not fully reflecting this in its own structures and operations.

A conference was held in 1979, in Clare College, Cambridge, with A. R. Peacocke, Dean and Director of Studies in Theology, and Hereward Cooke as the organisers. Peacocke's particular interest was science and faith. The theme was 'Technology', and speakers included Kenneth Adams, Ted Wickham, P. C. Schumacher of British Steel, and Colin Pritchard, formerly Director of the Society, Religion and Technology project. John Davis, who was involved with 'intermediate technology', described the accelerating pace of technological and consequential social change as 'bewildering'. Nearly every technological development, he suggested, could be used either for good or evil, and Christians needed to be engaged in analysis. Yet again, we might note how ICF's often unheeded prophetic voice was being raised at such an early moment. It was in 2020 that Tim Berners-Lee, recognised as the inventor of the World Wide Web, lamented the unforeseen ethical demise of the internet and argued in a BBC lecture that its biggest forward challenge was not a technological but a moral one. This was summarised by ICF's Chair at the time in its joint publication *Faith in Business Quarterly*.

ICF's involvement in Cambridge had links with other developments in the region. Mike Herbert, a Baptist minister and a full-time Industrial Chaplain with the Bishop of Peterborough's team, was involved in a 'stress in industry' cross-disciplinary group comprising managers, staff, chaplains and psychologists. A widely reported 'Festival of Work' was held at Norwich Cathedral. Among the speakers were Kenneth Adams and John Garnett of the Industrial Society. There was an exhibition, drama and an evening of folk singing. The event attracted people from the CBI and the TUC, but there were very few shop floor workers. The prophetic engagement was real, but limited.

Christian vocation in industry and commerce
The 1980s began with the organisation of another major conference. It was held in Oxford in 1980 and was on 'Christian Vocation in Industry and Commerce'. A high-level ICF research group had been doing the preparatory work for two years. The group included Peter Baelz, who was Regius Professor of Moral and Pastoral Theology, University of Oxford, and later became Dean of Durham Cathedral; John Adair, Professorial Fellow in Leadership Studies at Surrey University; and Robin Gill, Lecturer in Christian Ethics and Practical Theology, New College, Edinburgh. The conference was attended by 76 people, from management, trade unions,

education, chaplaincy, finance, medicine, the charitable sector, churches and industrial mission. In his presentation at the conference, Baelz spoke on the characteristics of a Christian vocation. Gill, in his paper, argued that the idea of vocation had been applied too narrowly by Christians, with the focus being on the caring professions. His view was that the idea of vocation could enrich all work even in a secular society. Margaret Brown, in another of the main papers, spoke on managers and Christian vocation. Adair's subject was vocation and creation. In small groups, a vision for industrial life was set out: co-operation, job enrichment, care for workers and concern for the community were prominent themes.

A year later, a major service (over a year of planning had been undertaken) took place at St Paul's Cathedral. The service was one of thanksgiving and intercession for industry and commerce. Companies and trade unions were encouraged to attend with flags and banners. The 2,200 people present heard a sermon by John Habgood, then Bishop of Durham. One of the London Anglican clergy deeply involved in this event was Malcolm Grundy. He had trained as an architect before studying theology and in the 1970s he joined the Sheffield Industrial Mission, becoming Senior Chaplain. While there he founded a training workshop for unemployed young adults. In 1980, he moved to the Diocese of London to be Director of Education and Community. He later became the Director of Avec, a consultancy agency for church and community work. Alongside the work for the service in St Paul's, Grundy wrote an article for the *ICF Quarterly* on 'Technology and the Future'. By contrast with those who concentrated on the hope held out in technology, he spoke of recent research which showed that rapidly expanding consumer societies were eating up reserves of energy and raw materials at a rate which would exhaust supplies within the lifetime of the next generation. The prophetic voice was again speaking with clarity, though we might lament that again it appeared to have lost the ear of those who might be able to act upon its warnings – it would be some decades before environmental issues were embraced by policy-makers with the same sense of urgency.

In order to take the work of the 1980 Oxford Conference forward, ICF launched a series of theme pamphlets. This new initiative was undertaken by John Davis, who took over from Hereward Cooke as Director in 1982 and wrote several of these on a range of subjects. Cooke became Priest-in-Charge of St Edmund's, Lombard Street, in the City of London. The ICF leadership was now 100 per cent lay. Davis had been a member of the Cambridge Inter-Collegiate Christian Union while a student. He was an Anglican and was seen as being able to relate to the whole spectrum of church-life. A chartered engineer by background, his experience included being Head of Products and Marketing Development for Shell International Petroleum, and Chairman and Chief Executive for groups of small Shell subsidiary companies. Part of his vision was for the expansion of local ICF groups. By this time membership had reduced to 550. In 1984, Davis oversaw the appointment of Regional Secretaries, who undertook this work on a voluntary basis. Davis was also interested in the European dimension. An Annual Lecture was given by Jack Peel, of the Social Affairs Directorate of the EEC, who had been a member of the TUC General Council. Peel criticised the British industrial relations system for having 'an opposing rather than a co-operative style'. He proposed changes along the lines of what was happening in other countries of Western Europe, where productivity was increasing faster than in Britain.

A prominent theme in the early 1980s was the problems caused by unemployment. In the 1970s, unemployment rates had been rising but with the Conservative Government led by Margaret Thatcher, which took power in 1979, there was a rapid rise to over three million out of work in 1983. Two Annual Lectures addressed the issue. Sir Richard O'Brien, Chairman of the Manpower Services Commission (MSC) and a supporter of ICF, spoke on 'Unemployment and the Christian Conscience'. He drew from work done by Margaret Thrall on Christian vocation today, and by Margaret Kane, author of *Gospel in Industrial Society* (1980) and Theological Consultant to Churches in the North East of England. O'Brien argued for a focus on the needs of young and disabled people, who were more likely to be unemployed than others. He drew on the work of William Temple, while noting that in Temple's time there was greater confidence about the place of Christianity in society. O'Brien argued – as had Temple – for the development of human potential. The MSC youth employment programme was commended by O'Brien: he rejected the term 'scroungers' being applied to the unemployed. The next Annual Lecture was given by Roy Grantham, General Secretary of the Association of Professional, Executive, Clerical and Computer Staff (APEX). Again, he spoke of the large numbers of unemployed, and drawing from Catholic social tradition – particularly Pope John Paul II's 1981 encyclical, *On Human Work* – he called for work to be placed at the centre of Christian theology.

However, there was concern within ICF that the impact of the churches in relation to industrial issues was continuing to decline. This seemed to be confirmed by a survey of which 4,000 copies were sent out and 600 were returned. Analysis of the results showed that few respondents considered there was a close connection between the churches and industrial and commercial life, although there was a desire for a better situation. John Davis took the opportunity to say that ICF wanted the:

> establishment of an understanding and a concern for industry and commerce in local churches throughout Britain, so that 'working life' may become a regular element in prayer, worship, fellowship and the teaching of congregations.

In addition, it wanted to encourage those committed to Christian thought and action in relation to industrial and commercial issues. As an example of where more could be done, ICF discussed a collection of papers written by Christian graduates. The feelings of unemployed graduates were highlighted: failure, depression, guilt and panic. From this, it was argued that churches could be more active in supporting graduates, both employed and unemployed, as well as others. David Sheppard, Bishop of Liverpool, contributed to the discussion, noting that the unemployment rate in Liverpool was 20 per cent, with many long-term unemployed. There was also a recognition of changing workplace patterns: trade unions were becoming weaker; more part-time work was in evidence; and self-employment was growing. Christian vocation had to take account of all these factors.

Faith, work and worship

In 1985, June Winfield, who was Industrial Chaplain to shops in London's West End, wrote for ICF on 'Faith, Work and Worship'. She took up the theme of 'consumerism', arguing that this 'perpetuates the selfish attitude of some people of satisfying their immediate needs, whatever the cost to others'. The 'worship' aspect was one that was highlighted in 1985 by the co-production of *Work in Worship*, an anthology of prayers, reading and hymns related to the world of work. This was published by Hodder & Stoughton, in association with the Oxford Institute for Church and Society. Cameron Butland, who compiled this, had worked in the City of London, and then became an ordinand at Ripon College. Alastair Redfern, who was his tutor, gave him encouragement in what was seen as work that bridged the gap between being Christians at work and at worship. ICF had also conducted a competition for hymns on work. A hymn, 'Our daily work', by Fred Pratt Green of Norwich, a Methodist minister and a prolific hymn-writer, was the winner. ICF guaranteed to the publisher the sale of 2,000 copies of *Work in Worship* and within two years that number had been sold.

The role of women as industrial chaplains and in the workplace did begin to be given greater attention from the mid-1980s. Ruth Etchells, the Principal of St John's College, Durham, was the first woman to deliver the Annual Lecture. Rachel Waterhouse, Chair of the Consumers' Association, was the second, in 1989. There was acknowledgement in the *Quarterly* that too few articles described women's perceptions of working life. Among the articles seeking to remedy this was one by Sheila Needham, on being a Christian managing director. Her firm was Needham Printers, and she described how it had grown from small beginnings to 27 staff and how values shaped the firm. In her work she had a Christian support group. She noted that research into the characteristics of successful managers was showing that many areas in which women were commonly seen to be strong, such as caring, sharing, listening, consulting and encouraging participation, were those connected with good management. Another article was by Brenda Cowderoy, on 'Women at Work', looking at changes from 1955 to 1985. She had studied at St Hugh's College, Oxford, and following that was called to the Bar. She became a legal adviser to the John Lewis Partnership and then General Secretary of the YMCA. Her article explored the implications of the rise in the number of women in paid employment to over 40 per cent of the workforce. In line with this, ICF was advertising scholarships for professional development opportunities for women, in conjunction with the Mary Macarthur Educational Trust, established in 1968 in memory of Macarthur, a Scottish suffragist.

Conservation and sustainability, which had emerged as ICF themes in the 1970s, continued to receive attention through the later 1980s. Although Malvern's concern for conservation tended to be overlooked, Charles Raven took forward what was later termed 'ecotheology'. One person who recognised the significance of this aspect of Malvern's discussions was David Arthur, who was a chartered accountant, originally from Scotland, and whose support for ICF led to his succeeding John Davis in 1986. David Arthur took the title of ICF National Secretary, rather than Director. He was committed to looking seriously at a whole range of issues, not least those of ecology and conservation, in relation to industrial society. John Davis had been editor of the *ICF Quarterly* along with his director role, but David Welbourn took on this role in 1986. Welbourn was for ten years an Industrial Chaplain in Norwich and then moved to Guildford as the Churches' Officer for Industry and Commerce with Surrey and North-East Hampshire Industrial Mission. Under Welbourn, the *Quarterly* continued to act as an important forum for ideas. On environmental questions, one of the articles was by Ken Addison, a professional engineer, who spoke from first-hand knowledge of the dangers of overdevelopment.

David Arthur believed that ICF's future lay in team-work. The central office now had only himself, the sole full-time employee, and John Bowmer, who was part time and looked after administration and membership. Bowmer's previous work had been for the Salvation Army, and prior to that he was a social worker. There was a small ICF office presence and library in St Katharine Cree, where Hugh Rom, a member of ICF, was now Priest-in-Charge. David Arthur looked to the Executive Committee members for their active involvement. There were 14 members, only two of whom were now clergy – David Welbourn and Malcolm Grundy. Peter Gardiner-Hill, who had experience as a managing director, took over from Kenneth Adams in chairing the committee. In addition, David Arthur wanted to develop further the role of the Regional Secretaries. The number grew to 18. Some were clergy, among them non-stipendiary clergy such as Mike Hammond in Norwich, who worked in personnel management. Others were lay, most of them Anglicans, such as Allan Chesnet, Operations Director of the Greater Manchester Employment Association. The first Baptist to be appointed was John Highley, a chemical engineer working for the National Coal Board in a research centre. Several Regional Secretaries had local lists of 20–30 people and local 'World of Work' groups met from time to time.

By this time, ICF had developed a clear identity as a membership organisation and so a key focus was the attraction of new members. In 1986, an advertisement in the *Church Times* produced a rapid increase from 316 to 852. However, it was subsequently noted that, out of 1,029 copies of the *Quarterly* being sent out, there were only 407 recipients who paid for it. The annual meeting of ICF members attracted about 60 people. Another initiative in this period was the launch of *MONDAY*, a tabloid-style newspaper. This was inserted into denominational newspapers such as the *Church Times, Church of England Newspaper, Universe, Baptist Times* and *Methodist Recorder*, and it was estimated that it reached half a million readers. However, costs were prohibitive, incurring an outlay of around £10,000 per issue without achieving any equivalent increase in subscription income. The age profile of ICF members was another problem. A survey showed that only 11 per cent were aged under forty. Partly in response to this, an ICF Young People's Project was launched. The chair of this was Malcolm Grundy, and the involvement of Hazel Sherman, a Baptist minister in Birmingham, together with Rob Frost, a young Methodist minister, meant that the project was thoroughly ecumenical. The aim was to help young people 'acquire an understanding of the spiritual nature of work'. ICF also participated in a conference at St Edmund Hall, Oxford, in 1988, on 'Creativity and Responsibility', for those working with young adults.

As we pause to look back over these years, ICF could be described as having adapted well to the new landscape in which it found itself. It had proved itself well capable of bringing together people from disparate walks of life, reminding them of their common identity as Christian believers, and generating insightful resources that expressed Christian faith and practice in the language of this new land. While always remaining a willing conversation partner, there seems little aspiration within these later conferences to become directly involved, as an organisation, in the operations of Church or State. Its supporters brought sufficient insight and experience for it to be able to speak with credibility, its scope was unusually broad, and it retained sufficient independence to speak with prophetic honesty and openness. The challenge for the years ahead would be whether, without such direct and structural ties to decision-makers and influencers, it could develop and maintain adequate channels of communication through which its message could still be heard. Although it might not have been described as such, with Studdert Kennedy and his network of missioners, Kirk had established an effective communications network in an age when there was little to rival the 'face-to-face' oratory and rhetoric at which Studdert Kennedy was so adept. We might remember that the BBC was only formed in 1922, did not produce anything near to a national radio broadcast until 1925 and did not receive its Royal Charter until 1927. Although Hopkinson's foray into the world of television might be one bold attempt, in subsequent years, ICF had never really managed to establish anything like its equivalent. Another issue that had already begun to re-emerge is that, with no obvious institutional role, how could it remain financially sustainable? While Donald Coggan's earlier description of ICF as 'catalytic' may have been insightful and made with positive intent, those with a knowledge of chemistry might note that a catalyst is the participant that enables the reaction without becoming part of or being recognised in what emerges.

The future of ICF by the end of the 1980s seemed to lie in partnerships with other bodies and movements. Some of the groups featured in the *Quarterly* were the Institute of Business Ethics, the Industry Matters Churches' Group, the London Institute for Contemporary Christianity, the Shaftesbury Project (directed by Roy McCloughry), the Oxford Institute for Church and Society, the Jubilee Centre (led by Michael Schluter), the

Carpenters' Trust, St Martin-in-the-Fields Centre for the World of Work, and the New Economics Foundation, of which John Davis was a trustee. In some cases, these connections meant that ICF found new speakers and writers. By 1990, 33 theme pamphlets had been produced. There was also some joint publication with the Church of England's Board for Social Responsibility. The most important partnership was with the 'God on Monday' project at the Evangelical Anglican Ridley Hall, Cambridge. For some years this had been developing in the mind of Hugo de Waal, the Principal, and it was launched in 1988. The *ICF Quarterly* reported that the Director was Richard Higginson, a graduate of St John's College, Cambridge, who had been Tutor in Ethics at Cranmer Hall and St John's College, Durham. People from the world of business began to come to study at Ridley, taking part in special courses. Topics included success and failure, work and unemployment, the role of companies in the community, crisis management, rewards and incentives, profit and added value, industry and the environment, and marketing. The aim, which was fully in line with that of ICF, was to bring Christian perspectives to bear on these issues. Under the auspices of 'God on Monday' (which was to become 'Faith in Business'), David Welbourn began to compile material on the theology of work, perhaps an indication of what this partnership would come to signify for the vision of ICF.

Reflection

Returning to the thoughts in the opening of this chapter, writing of his long experience as a priest in the East End of London, Kenneth Leech has an important challenge to ICF and contextual ministry for the church today. He ends his book, *Through Our Long Exile: Contextual Theology and the Urban Experience* with these words:

> As Christians enter the twenty-first century, they do so as exiles, strangers and pilgrims, aliens in a strange land. They will need to learn strategies of survival, and to sing the songs of Zion in the midst of Babylon.

He believed that the churches had yet to come to terms with a multicultural Britain or, for that matter, with spirituality and community in a global urbanised society. Using his own experience of ministry, Leech explored the importance of contextual theology for a Church on the margin.

Leech recounts that this is where he has lived and worked, and where he has sought to be a theologian who reflects upon the word of God in a specific context. He notes that the history of the East End is part of the recent world history of urbanisation, which has taken us to the place where more than 90 per cent of the British people can be described as urbanised. In the East End, population increase has taken place alongside social polarisation and economic dislocation. As both internal and external migration has taken place, he argues that the world of settled, static communities is gone forever.

Urban decay, decline and division mark the recent history of the context from which Leech was writing. A decline in population was mirrored by a decline in manufacturing industry and infrastructure, with resulting social problems and social polarisation. The Canary Wharf development with accompanying expensive property has exacerbated the situation. The greatest inequality is seen in health, where the death rate in the East End is 14 per cent higher and the rate of illness 27 per cent higher than the rest of England and Wales.

Against this background, Leech sets his agenda for urban theology. The following are some of the items he identifies: How do we judge cities theologically? How do we address economic justice – the gap between rich and poor; justice for immigrants in employment and opportunity; churches as expressions of community; finding value and dignity in the face of unemployment; addressing issues of pollution, health and housing; empowering the voiceless; and learning from Christian experience in other world cities?

Leech challenges a sterile theology restricted to discussion within the academy and encourages us to be engaged in contextual thinking, which struggles with and reflects upon a specific situation in the light of our faith tradition. His questions are: What is going on? Where are we? What are the forces that shape us and threaten us? Where are the points of leverage and areas of hope? These are questions that can helpfully reframe the vision of organisations such as ICF for a contemporary age.

The questions that Leech asks develop an agenda for urban spirituality which encompasses: the materialistic – reality of human need; the compassionate – suffering together; the passionate – expressing anger; awe and amazement in the face of a strange and alien humanity; inner silence – self-reflection; and a sense of hope and liberation. He looks for a rediscovery of a prophetic voice, warning that a pragmatic or servant church has replaced the prophetic church.

This is a challenging agenda for ICF at the end of the twentieth century and as it moves through the twenty-first century.

Chapter 7

Hope, disappointment and a fresh direction

As The Industrial Christian Fellowship (ICF) entered the 1990s, the hope of the Executive was that there could be a new period of expansion. In 1991, Roger Holloway was appointed Director and he anticipated the future with optimism and with considerable energy. The aim that was talked about was how to restore ICF to its 'place at the top table'. With a range of other Christian organisations now being strongly committed to the area of faith at work, this was an ambitious – and as it turned out over-ambitious – agenda.

It might be argued that Holloway had recognised many of the issues that have been observed through recent chapters. ICF's message and vision were as vital as ever, but it had lost the connections that could give them the significance they deserved. One element that it had perhaps neglected was establishing any alternative means through which it could speak into the public square. This in turn would perpetuate the ever-present issue of financial and organisational sustainability. But Holloway embarked upon his role with a clear strategy for how these realities might be addressed.

A range of conferences, seminars and lectures were held in the first half of the 1990s, and publications continued, but it was evident that the aim of raising a substantial amount of money was not going to be fulfilled. Roger Holloway announced in 1996 that he was resigning as Director. The Executive had to work out a strategy for a future in which there was no possibility of having any paid staff. It even seemed for a time that the entire enterprise might come to an end. The membership had dropped to a low point of 110. However, a partnership with the Ridley Hall Foundation in Cambridge to publish a new journal gave ICF a higher profile and membership rose to 230. This chapter describes the twists and turns of this challenging and dramatic decade in the Fellowship's life.

New initiatives

A major ICF initiative in July 1991 was a four-day conference at Malvern, which was intended to set out a vision for the future in a way that was similar to what had happened in 1941 at the first Malvern Conference. Preparation for Malvern '91 began in 1989. It was agreed that among the main themes to be studied would be citizenship and the democratic process, the socio-economic traditions of Europe, philosophy, culture, science and technology, and the environment. The organisers were able to enlist the involvement of Archbishop Robert Runcie, who was the President of ICF, Cardinal Basil Hume, and Bernard Thorogood, who represented the Free Churches. By the time of the conference, Runcie had retired. However, George Carey, the new Archbishop of Canterbury, agreed to preach at the conference, and John Habgood, the Archbishop of York, also gave an address. Among the almost 400 people who were part of the event, a range of denominations was represented, from Western and Eastern Europe and the non-Western world. Most were from Christian traditions but there were also some Jews and Muslims present. John Bell of the Iona Community led the worship.

Several major concerns emerged as the conference proceeded. Under citizenship, there was an affirmation that Britain, and Europe more widely, needed a body of common values, while at the same time there was a need to ensure that each person's unique identity was recognised. The concept of unity in diversity was explored, and George Carey proposed that Christianity had a model to offer to society. Edward Heath, the former Conservative Prime Minister, outlined possibilities for Europe which drew from the past and looked to the future and which warned against the idea of 'Fortress Europe'. Other speakers, too, wished to see 'open frontiers'. On the issue of the environment, it was agreed that the Christian perspective was that human beings were stewards of God's world, with a particular responsibility for the environment, levels of pollution and the use of non-renewable resources. In all the discussions, the question that was asked was: 'What kind of world do we want to build?' Echoing its long-standing convictions, ICF saw the conference as setting out a pathway in which every sphere of life could be informed by a set of principles and moral values based on Christian teaching, to the ultimate benefit of everyone. It remained especially committed to finding what was most beneficial within the world of business and commerce for employees, management, shareholders, suppliers, customers and the whole community.

David Arthur, the former Secretary, was at Malvern, having attended in the previous week a major Roman Catholic conference in Liverpool which marked the centenary of *Rerum Novarum* ('of revolutionary change'), an encyclical issued by Pope Leo XIII in 1891. This explored the rights and duties of capital and labour, and included a call for the great needs of the working classes to be addressed. It became a foundational text of Roman Catholic social teaching. David Arthur was encouraged that at both the Liverpool and Malvern conferences large numbers were present, with good proportions of younger people at each. It was noted with some delight that, in the keynote speech in Liverpool, Derek Worlock, the city's Roman Catholic Archbishop, gave considerable attention to aspects of the world of work. Worlock, who worked closely with David Sheppard, the Anglican Bishop of Liverpool, stated that he wanted to see an 'ecumenical adult Christian worker movement'. ICF also drew attention to the 'Workers' Charter' that was issued in 1991 by Pope John Paul II. It felt that once again there was a wider appetite for the issues and agendas that were so central to its own purpose.

It is not surprising that in this context of optimism, as it began to look towards the twenty-first century, hopes were placed in the leadership for ICF that could emanate from Roger Holloway. He had studied at Selwyn College, Cambridge, and then embarked on a long career in the wine business. In his spiritual journey he was indebted to Robert Runcie. Holloway trained for Anglican ministry through the Southwark Ordination Course and was ordained an Anglican priest in 1981. Alongside his business, which took him to different parts of the world, he served as a 'worker-priest'. He was a member at St John's Cathedral in Hong Kong and then the Anglican church in Tokyo. In 1988, he returned to London and became Vicar at St Margaret's, Westminster, taking his turn at prayers in the House of Commons and getting to know political figures. He had the ability to make friends in high places but was not always adept at fostering warm relationships in other contexts. Holloway insisted that ministers in secular employment were not 'second class', and when he was appointed it was agreed that he would continue to undertake duties as an Anglican priest, and also retain a number of his non-executive directorships and consultancies, some of which involved travel to the Far East. Holloway saw his 'foothold in commerce' as important.

In seeking the way forward, Holloway's strongly held view was that ICF should move away from its long history of direct involvement in the workplace and embrace a new calling: to be 'an intellectual power house, a resource for those seriously interested in the issues of Faith and Work'. He also saw its potential – and this was typical of Holloway's way of thinking – as an 'influencer of influencers'. In order to achieve this, he became involved in meetings connected with Industrial Mission and the Industrial and Economic Affairs Committee of the Church of England's Board for Social Responsibility. Through Holloway, ICF articulated a fresh aim, which was 'to change attitudes to the world of work by helping people to find a fuller sense of God's purpose in their working lives'. In particular, there was a desire to help Christians 'realise that in the world of work they serve both God and neighbour, and that Faith, Work and Worship are all one'. Part of the new initiative was a commitment to looking at contemporary moral dilemmas in the workplace; providing new resources for churches to support people in their working lives; and showing the importance of all people's work in generating wealth for the common good. These new initiatives required additional funding, and an ambitious plan was set out, with a target to raise £45,000 over and above current income, in order to launch them.

Ways of communicating

Some of the Fellowship's publishing work continued, but with a significant emphasis on improving the graphic style and quality to one that better engaged this new context. The *ICF Quarterly*, edited by David Welbourn, carried major articles, which on occasion were critical of past ICF emphases. For example, Antony Wood, Director of Understanding Industry, considered that too many of its publications in the past had been 'wary of business life'. Although that was an overstatement, ICF now made clear its commitment to business and enterprise. It commended the work of Charles Green on 'the Christian in business'. Green, a senior banking figure, was Vice-Chairman of Business in the Community, Vice-Chairman of the Anglican Board for Social Responsibility, and Chairman of the Industrial and Economic Affairs Committee. He was also active in the Church Urban Fund, which was set up in response to the report *Faith in the City*. ICF, however, did not want to be seen as involved only with the Church of England. The *Quarterly* was enthusiastic about the 'splendid report' from the Methodist Conference, 'The Ministry of the People of God in the World'.

The themes covered in the *Quarterly* and other ICF publications, such as the theme pamphlets, included: stress at work; the role of money; self-interest in business; ethical investment; take-over bids; and market forces. By the early 1990s, 54 theme pamphlets had been produced. David Welbourn's *Faith and Work: Bridging the Theological Gap* was particularly crucial. Welbourn was concerned to probe aspects of Christian thinking about involvement at work. In his writing he outlined the way work had been seen as a place of witness, as a means of earning money, as giving opportunities to contribute to society, and as an environment for showing Christian qualities. All these he saw as having merit, but in his view the most important dimension to be communicated was that work was within the purpose of God. He was disappointed by a book produced by David Adam, Vicar of Holy Island, entitled *Celtic Prayers about Work*. Most of the prayers were about everyday life, not specifically work. Joy Williamson, who taught economics and business, was concerned to analyse work in relation to 'business values'. She argued that, while many thought the market was secular and value-free, that was not the case. Values needed to be acknowledged. Though perhaps not recognised at the time, Williamson could be seen as an early advocate of what might now be described as a postmodern approach to issues of identity and culture.

Other ways through which ICF communicated were regional seminars, organised in conjunction with its 19 regional representatives, and the Annual Lecture. As an example of speakers Holloway drew in, the 1993 lecture was delivered by Sir Jeremy Morse, Chancellor of Bristol University, who had been Chairman of Lloyd's Bank. In his address, which was attended by 100 people, he called for more truth in political life. One regional seminar, organised in the Diocese of Peterborough, was attended by 150 people, where Tim Boswell MP, the Minister for Rural Affairs at the Ministry of Agriculture, Fisheries and Food, was the keynote speaker. The Fellowship also took an active part in supporting lectures and seminars organised by other groups. There was interest in the Ridley Hall Foundation (now 'Faith in Business') which prior to 1992 was known as 'God on Monday'. The Foundation held a number of seminar weeks in the first half of 1993 – on leadership, success and failure in business, and innovation. Another connection for ICF was with Hull University's lectures on 'Theological Understanding of Industrial Society'. The prime mover was Peter Sedgwick, a Senior Lecturer at the university who in 1992 produced what ICF described as 'a deep and serious book', *The Enterprise Culture*.

His writings for ICF included *Capitalism Triumphant?* In 1996, Sedgwick became Policy Officer at the Anglican Board for Social Responsibility.

International perspectives

One aspect of industry that had gathered pace in the previous decades was its international dimensions and structures, and while this was not entirely absent previously, we can detect within Holloway's era a clear extension of ICF's vision to include business links overseas. Continuing its tradition of multidisciplinary conferences, in 1992 the Executive began to plan a major gathering at the University of Kent, Canterbury. This took place two years later and would focus especially, although not exclusively, on Japanese business and Britain. The title of the conference was 'The Global Workplace'. Two of the main speakers from Britain were John Habgood, Archbishop of York, and Baron Young of Graffham, who had been the Secretary of State for Trade and Industry. Representatives of Japanese industry, such as Shōichi Saba of Toshiba, also contributed to what was seen as a very successful conference, attracting 100 participants. A gift from the Daiwa Anglo-Japanese Foundation, which had been established in 1988 to promote closer links between Japan and Britain, enabled documents from the conference to be widely circulated. One influence on ICF in its pan-national links in this period was John Atherton, of Manchester Cathedral and Manchester Business School, who encouraged global thinking about stewardship of creation and social wellbeing. Yet again we might notice how ICF found itself in the vanguard of policy development – it was only in 1986 that Nissan had opened its production plant in Sunderland, described 30 years later in the North East's *Evening Chronicle* as a move that 'transformed the North East and UK manufacturing as a whole'.

ICF had sustained interest in European-wide relationships, with the European Community described as an outcome of 'inspired co-operation between two nations with fearsome military traditions, France and Germany'. It was acknowledged that Britain often appeared to stand aloof from the European debate, but ICF expressed a belief that Christians could have a distinctive role. One of the pro-European figures whose thinking about involvement in industry was drawn on at the time was Sir Fred Catherwood, a Member of the European Parliament. Catherwood, who stood in the Reformed tradition, emphasised the importance of the work ethic. However, Sir Hugh Beach, a former military officer who became Chairman of the Church Army, claimed in the *ICF Quarterly* that Catherwood's 'rather ferocious work ethic' went beyond St Paul's teaching.

There was concern that poverty might be seen as a sign of a poor work ethic, when in reality deeper structural factors were present. Patricia Hewitt, who had helped to establish the Commission on Social Justice in Britain, gave the 1995 ICF Annual Lecture, held that year at Lambeth Palace. Her topic was 'Social Justice in a Global Economy'. This attracted more people than any other recent Annual Lecture.

People and possibilities

In 1994, the Executive members recorded their view that there were 'enormous possibilities' ahead, based on what had been achieved in the previous two years. In 1992, Roger Holloway had secured the services of Lord (Bernard) Weatherill, until recently Speaker of the House of Commons, and now a cross-bench peer in the House of Lords, to be the Chairman of the Council. For Holloway this marked an important step in expanding the Fellowship's national role. In the same year he proposed that it should adopt a new name, the Industry Churches Forum. Holloway preferred Forum to Fellowship. The change of name would, he believed, describe the organisation's position as a bridge between industry in its widest sense and the Christian Church. In practice, however, the change was not widely accepted and the name Industrial Christian Fellowship continued to be commonly used. Key people on the Executive at this stage were Peter Gardiner-Hill, who chaired the committee, along with Clive Wright, who had been Director of Public Affairs for Esso and a consultant with Arco Chemical Europe Inc., Ewan Harper, an educationalist, Terry Drummond, an Urban Industrial Missioner in Croydon, Canon Malcolm Grundy, who was the author in 1992 of *An Unholy Conspiracy: The Scandal of the Separation of Church and Industry Since the Reformation*, David Welbourn, and Ronald Ind, the Honorary Treasurer.

Roger Holloway was able to capitalise on the appointment of Lord Weatherill to attract new and influential members to the ICF Council, a body which was now much smaller than previously. Baroness (Judith) Wilcox, who was chair of the National Consumers' Council, brought her entrepreneurial experience in the fishing industry. Emma Nicholson MP, another new member, had been a Director of the Save the Children Fund. Someone who joined the Council and would remain involved in ICF over the succeeding decades was Frank Field MP. In 1993, lectures Field gave in Durham on social policy – its philosophy, future and imperatives – attracted national attention. Field's vision was to help the poor to get off welfare and into employment, and he denounced what he argued was the calculated creation by the Conservative Government of an impoverished and excluded underclass. There was widespread agreement that Field, who was MP for Birkenhead, an area of very high unemployment, understood the ravages of poverty better than almost any other MP. Alongside that, his Christian faith, as a High Anglican, evidently influenced his concerns. Another significant appointment to the Council was Canon Geoffrey Brown, who since 1985 had been Vicar of St Martin-in-the-Fields and who had brought this famous church back from the brink of bankruptcy. His skills proved vital in the challenges that yet lay ahead.

In looking at possibilities for the 1990s and beyond, ICF was indebted to both long-standing and new members. John Davis, ICF Director in the early 1980s, remained involved, and encouraged a strong commitment to ecology. He wrote one of the theme pamphlets, *The Green Imperative*. He also wrote for the New Economics Foundation on sustainable development, which for him had to include 'greening business'. This was against the background of the establishment of the European Environment Agency (1990) and the United Nations Framework Convention on Climate Change (1992). Kenneth Adams, a former Chair of the Executive, also continued to support ICF's aims. He was one of three main speakers at a conference in Birmingham on 'Ethics in Business', which attracted 130 participants. Another speaker was Mark Santer, Bishop of Birmingham. Links were renewed with Cadbury's, which had historically taken an interest in ICF. Among the new voices were: Wendy Brooker, the first Anglican woman priest to be on the Executive; Ruth Badger, from the Anglican Board for Social Responsibility; John Lovatt, Managing Director of a medium-sized ceramics firm in the Potteries, who became ICF Secretary and wrote on 'Jesus in the Workplace: Towards a Better Theology of Work'; and Peter Selby, William Leech Professorial Fellow in Applied Christian Theology, Durham, and then Bishop of Worcester. At a weekend consultation on wealth creation, at St George's House, Windsor, two of three principal speakers were members of the Executive, Clive Wright and Malcolm Grundy.

With the end of communist power in Eastern Europe, there was considerable discussion of the opportunities and problems within the capitalist system. Peter Sedgwick was one of those who urged ICF and other bodies to move away from the view that an enterprise culture was the same as 'naked individual competitiveness'. He was often to be found arguing that emerging economic opportunities should be embraced. There were others, however, who were cautious about an emphasis on individual endeavour and the market, and wished to affirm the social tradition that had informed the Fellowship's formative vision. In 1992, the Government closed 31 of the 50 deep coal mines across the country, with the loss of 30,000 mining jobs and as many as 70,000 associated jobs. The *ICF Quarterly* covered the repercussions of this drastic closure programme, with the focus at the time being on the issue of unemployment rather than on the environmental impact of fossil fuels. To encourage broader thinking among younger people about these and other contemporary issues, ICF invited theological students to submit essays on major themes and offered prizes of £500. These were won by Paul Weary, a Methodist finishing his ministerial training at Wesley College, Bristol, who looked at the history and relevance of a work ethic, and Nigel Sinclair, an Anglican student at Cranmer Hall, Durham, who wrote on 'What has Christianity to do with economics?' David Ford, Regius Professor of Divinity at Cambridge University, judged the entries.

Despite the hopes for the future, and despite the energy put into seeking new sources of funding, it was clear by 1995 that capital was being used up at an alarming rate. The target to raise £45,000 had been set in the expectation of expansion. However, by 1995 only £19,500 had been raised, and the financial situation deteriorated. At one stage the annual loss was £43,000. There were predictions that the 'potentially disastrous' situation, as Clive Wright put it, might mean closure within three years. At the 1995 AGM, attended by 31 members, the serious situation was addressed. Holloway spoke of his gratitude to the Executive, to Lord Weatherill, and to Anthony Loehnis, a former Director of the Bank of England, who had approached City institutions about ICF's needs. Despite all the efforts, the Fellowship's work was not proving attractive to potential backers. Holloway spoke of the past year as one of the most difficult in his 38 years of working life. He announced that he would be leaving the organisation in 1996, as would John Bowman, the Membership Secretary. It seemed there was no possibility of being able to have paid staff in future. Once again, ICF had proved its effectiveness in pursuing its far-reaching vision, and yet seemed to founder on its inability to generate the resources needed to sustain its endeavours. Hope had given way to disappointment.

The Fellowship was standing at a crossroads, and facing a choice that confronts many aspirational organisations at a time of crisis. This was not simply a matter of 'change or die' – no one could question Holloway's level of ambition, or his creative endeavours to return the organisation to the place that its founders had always perceived for it. But there comes a point when it has to be accepted that members of any organisation cannot be simply recruited into another scheme, no matter how honourable and worthwhile, which they simply do not have the capacity to sustain. In such circumstances, the danger is that the focus becomes the resources that are unavailable rather than what can be done with those that are. At such times, vision needs to be faithfully defined by an honest recognition and gracious acceptance of the capabilities and capacities that the community has to offer. Enterprising Christians may often acknowledge their belief in the 'Body of Christ' in which 'every member has its part', yet they can often require of that body a level of performance that its members cannot realistically achieve. ICF was happy to accept that those who had been prompted to align themselves with its cause would be those among whom God could work to bring the next chapter of its life into being. A survey of members had shown there was a wish for the *Quarterly* and significant lectures to continue and there was support for some merger or alliance with a like-minded organisation.

Preserving the core activities

In April 1996, Roger Holloway wrote to the regional representatives to report on the current deliberations of the Executive and the Council. His letter was headed 'ICF: The Future'. He spoke of hard thinking that had taken place about 'how it would be possible for ICF to continue in the much colder climate'. The new aim was 'to preserve our core activities on a much smaller budget'. He reported that ICF representatives had entered into discussions with some of those involved in the Ridley Hall Foundation (RHF). Holloway had hopes for a full merger with RHF, but the RHF management team did not see this as right for them. Discussion then focused on how the *ICF Quarterly* or a successor journal might fit into the life of both organisations. This could in consequence mean increased journal circulation, perhaps with David Welbourn continuing as editor. Holloway also hoped that ICF would be able to continue with its 'splendid liturgical work', which – through Welbourn and others – was being produced. The Fellowship's main resource in this area was *Work in Worship*. There were also complications at the time about the continued use of St Katharine Cree, but Holloway was keen that either this location or somewhere else would continue to provide a London base.

   In the meantime, discussions with RHF, in particular with its Director Richard Higginson, were continuing. Clive Wright wrote to Higginson in April 1996 to confirm what had been said in a previous visit, that he believed Higginson's 'painstaking and patient efforts have had success

– not dramatic or high profile but positive and real nevertheless'. Wright considered that ICF could learn from this and his preference was for some pooling of resources. The profile of RHF was arguably higher than Wright suggested. The seminars at Ridley Hall were popular and ICF recommended Higginson's book *Called to Account* (1993) for the pioneering way in which way it showed the relevance of every major doctrine of Christian faith to the business world. Higginson followed this in 1996 with *Transforming Leadership: A Christian Approach to Management*. In May 1996, he sought advice from the RHF management team about a partnership with ICF in the publication of a good-quality journal. RHF was chaired by Graham Cray, the Principal of Ridley Hall. The management team agreed to consider any forthcoming proposal. It was recognised by the RHF team that the *ICF Quarterly* was the best publication in the 'faith and work' field.

On the part of ICF, the decision was made to continue the Annual Lecture, and to share the *Quarterly* publication with the Ridley Hall Foundation, with a £5,000 per year grant for three years, and for their representation on the editorial and management teams. It was felt by members that communication by lectures and publications was crucial for ICF. The last *ICF Quarterly* was in winter 1995/96, and the first issue of a new journal, *Faith in Business Quarterly* (*FiBQ*), appeared in March 1997. This was introduced as a journal of the Ridley Hall Foundation and ICF (Industry Churches Forum). The editorial team changed over time but the aim was always to have representation from both partners. Editors included Richard Higginson, whose role was central, David Murray from RHF, and David Welbourn and John Lovatt from ICF. The RHF Council of Reference included Kenneth Adams and Clive Wright, who were connected with both organisations, and James Allcock (British Gas) and Alan Spall (ICI), as well as some from academia, such as David Ford, Regius Professor of Divinity at Cambridge.

Although a new partnership had been put in place, it was not certain what future lay ahead for ICF itself. It seemed at one stage in 1997 that the work might come to an end. However, at the AGM on 18 June 1997, with 27 members present (and 34 apologies for absence), a way forward was mapped out. Reports were given of what was described by the Chairman, Canon Bernard Brown, as a 'reorganisation'. Brown was committed to international links in the field of faith and work, and was a trustee of a French mission dedicated to ecumenical fellowship between British and French Christians endeavouring to relate the Church to industry. He gave details to the meeting of a working party which over the previous few months had been seeking to find ways that would best preserve ICF's core activities. The working party, chaired by Lord Weatherill, comprised Bernard Brown, Geoffrey Brown, Denis Claringbull, a recently retired Senior Industrial Chaplain from the Birmingham Diocese, Terry Drummond, Michael Fass, who was about to become the presiding moderator of Christians in Secular Ministry (CHRISM), Edmund Flood, a Roman Catholic monk at Ealing Abbey, and John Raymond. The outcome on 18 June was that a new Executive was put in place. Geoffrey Brown became Chairman, Terry Drummond the Treasurer, and Sylvia Mead the Secretary. The name Industry Churches Forum gave way to the original Industrial Christian Fellowship.

In this period of change, the commitment of ICF to public lectures remained strong. Sir Andrew Large, Chairman of the Securities and Investment Board, the precursor of the Financial Conduct Authority, delivered a lecture in November 1996. He was later Deputy Governor of the Bank of England. In 1997, a lecture was given by Frank Field. With the new Labour Government, he became Minister for Welfare Reform, and he addressed the subject of 'The Evolution of Welfare'. It was Tony Blair's hope that Field would bring fresh thinking to this area. After his departure, Roger Holloway was elected Preacher (Chaplain) to Gray's Inn. The ICF base moved from St Katharine Cree to St Martin-in-the-Fields, with Geoffrey Brown's encouragement. As Chair of the Executive, Brown saw ICF becoming 'a partnership of working people concerned with a multiplicity of issues'. The *Faith in Business Quarterly* became the vehicle for wider coverage of this 'multiplicity'. An early editorial in *FiBQ* commented on an ICF Annual Lecture by John Monks, TUC General Secretary, and found Monks' vision for trade unions and society to be 'inspiring'. Monks spoke of his Methodist background and mindset, stating: 'We accept the challenges of change in a trade union spirit which stems largely from the Christian demands of justice, solidarity and compassion.' It was a view which, expressed in John Wesley's terms, warmed the heart of those who received it.

Renewal as a membership organisation

At a meeting of its members in 2000, which among other things looked at the change of direction since 1997, there was a recognition that ICF had 'renewed itself as a membership organisation' over the previous three years. The view was that much had already been achieved, and the organisation was now in a stronger position to tackle the work that remained to be done. Alongside the publishing role in partnership with the Ridley Hall

Foundation, a newsletter for ICF members was launched, featuring events and news from faith and work organisations, some brief theological pieces, especially on the theology of work, and correspondence. No salaries were now being paid and financial stability returned. The Executive learned how to work together in this new era, with Geoffrey Brown giving able leadership. Michael Fass became Vice-Chairman, with Terry Drummond continuing as Treasurer and Sylvia Mead as Secretary. Other committee members were Denis Claringbull, Edmund Flood, Anthony King, John Lovatt, John Raymond and Carol Williams, an Anglican priest in Buckinghamshire and former British Gas manager.

Anthony King and John Raymond were two of the remaining ICF regional representatives who were able to maintain a membership base within their respective localities. Raymond had developed a particularly active network in Bedfordshire, where he was also a local councillor. While working for the Scott Bader Company in Wellingborough, he had been key in the planning and organisation of a major conference in 1995, which was a joint initiative between Scott Bader, ICF and the Diocese of Peterborough. From this, the diocese developed its People at Work programme which was sustained over a number of years, including an online resource at a time when such things were still relatively novel. Raymond brought significant passion to ICF's work, not least because during his working life he had experienced the best and worst of business practices, which strengthened his resolve to see a significant voice for Christian ethics and values within the world of employment. King had recently retired from parish ministry where he had demonstrated a passion for relating faith to the world beyond the church doors. Although one of the less 'upfront' members of the emerging Executive, he brought a thoroughness and attention to detail that would become increasingly significant in the years that followed. Another key member of the group was Terry Drummond, with a background in the Church Army and now working as Social Responsibility Officer in the Diocese of Southwark. Drummond pioneered a number of effective partnerships between the faith and statutory sectors, particularly in the London Borough of Croydon, and brought a network of significant contacts and potential partners. He was also a prolific reader, and his book reviews generated a significant amount of content for many subsequent newsletters.

The link established with the Ridley Hall Foundation meant that the various events it organised attracted a number of ICF members. In 1997, RHF held a consultation on the stakeholder economy. Within this consultation, and later in *FiBQ*, there was reflection on corporate social responsibility (CSR), a term first used in the USA in the 1950s. The term and the concept behind it had been slow to catch on in Britain and only achieved widespread acceptance by UK business in the 1990s. CSR went hand in hand with recognition of companies' responsibilities to various different stakeholder groups. Also in 1997, an exploratory RHF seminar for Christians in the field of consultancy proved very popular. Out of this, an ongoing group was formed, with members of the group agreeing to spend 24 hours together at Ridley Hall three times a year. ICF's concern to work in co-operation with other agencies that had similar goals was being reflected in the scope of the events detailed in the ICF *Newsletter*. These included MODEM, a national and ecumenical Christian network seeking to initiate dialogue between exponents of leadership, organisation, spirituality and ministry, and CABE, the Christian Association of Business Executives, with which Clive Wright was heavily involved.

FiBQ featured a range of writers and topics. David Welbourn wrote a number of articles. There was a commitment to exploring biblical perceptions of work, vision, leadership, competition and success. Through *FiBQ* and other connections the ecumenical scope of ICF's work was broadened. John Ellis, who was appointed the first-ever Secretary for business and economic affairs for the Methodist Church in the UK, was a contributor to *FiBQ*. There was also an international reach, for example through Stephen Green, an ordained Anglican who was Group Treasurer of the Hongkong and Shanghai Banking Corporation (better known as HSBC), and Professor Prabhu Guptara of Union Bank of Switzerland, who addressed the issue of how to confront wrong in the world. Another issue that came to the fore was spirituality and business. It was recognised that this was a current topic in the business world that required analysis. David Welbourn was positive about the interest in spirituality. However, David Murray, another *FiBQ* editor, who was a management consultant, was concerned about anti-Christian developments in workplace spirituality. Dermot Tredget, a Benedictine monk who was a facilitator of residential workshop retreats, wrote for *FiBQ* explaining and applying Benedictine spirituality.

As ICF looked forward to entering a new century and looked back on a very turbulent decade in its history, the Executive Committee felt that the Fellowship had come through the crisis and that there were some grounds for optimism. There was encouragement that the readership of *FiBQ* was increasing. The partnership with RHF was seen as a major commitment, and with ICF's improved financial situation it was also possible to produce relevant worship material, offer grants and loans for projects in the field of faith and work, undertake research, and co-operate ecumenically. At ICF's last Annual General Meeting of the twentieth century, in November 1999, held at St Martin-in-the-Fields, Lord Weatherill affirmed the ongoing contribution of the Fellowship and spoke of his personal commitment to Christian fellowship in the place of work – in his case the House of Lords and the Palace of Westminster. Geoffrey Brown commended the Executive and the members as a whole for the team spirit that had now developed. Secretarial support was starting to be given to the Executive by Ann Wright, who was to prove increasingly valuable.

Looking back over this period, it would be fair to say that ICF had now abandoned any expression of Holloway's honourable attempt to regain its 'place at the top table'. It had become lighter on its feet, responsive to opportunity, but retained that unstinting belief that there is no aspect of life about which the message of Christ has nothing to say. For all that, numerically it was a fraction of what it once was. But for such a relatively small cohort of people, there were some very significant individuals within its ranks representing an eclectic and diverse mix of roles and responsibility. What they had in common was a sense of shared Christian identity, a genuine appreciation of an organisation that could take them seriously as disciples of Jesus within the positions that they held, and an environment where that tangible bond of Christian fellowship enabled honest, gracious and productive explorations of their differences. Irrespective of its scale of operation, ICF had managed to retain the basic principle that had always defined it as unique.

What was markedly different in its emerging mindset was that the Fellowship no longer sought to express the reign of Christ through some defined authority structure, around which economic and political affairs should coalesce, but rather through the prayerful enabling of the Spirit, guiding those in all walks of life to seek above all things the Kingdom of God. Though the language of the Spirit can sometimes be too thoughtlessly attached to religious endeavour, there seemed a genuine sense of openness, and perhaps a necessary humility, as they sought God's purposes for the way ahead. For all its grand aspirations, ICF had often returned in its early days to a call for earnest prayer as it sought to offer healing to a broken and despairing society, and it was through prayerful and reflective conversation that its Executive Committee now plotted its course. Their shared conviction was that this would continue to be built around the needs, aspirations and resources of its members.

During 1999, a plan for the future was developed, with the intention of looking at how it might be implemented in the coming years. The constructive work done on this owed a great deal to two residential 24-hour meetings of the Executive. This was proving to be the most effective way to conduct business. It was heartening for the Executive to hear that *FiBQ* subscribers had now reached 400, making it a viable publication in its own right. ICF was represented on the Editorial Board of *FiBQ* by John Lovatt, and Anthony King was joining the Steering Committee. Another channel of communication and commentary was the ICF *Newsletter*. In addition to the subscribed members who received it, others were interested, and 500 copies were being circulated four times a year. From a low point in membership of 110, steady growth had taken place over three years. Geoffrey Brown as Chairman and John Lovatt as Membership Secretary had worked together to contact lapsed members, and several had returned. There was a very welcome increase in the number of younger, lay members who were in full-time work. Membership by 2000 reached 233, of whom 142 were lay members, 74 were clergy and 17 were bishops. It was anticipated that the Fellowship would move increasingly towards being a largely lay-oriented organisation, with its resources directed to those employed in all areas of business.

A reflection:

Perhaps the experience of ICF in the 1980s and 1990s should raise questions about the focus of its mission, the composition of its leadership, and the roles of the people it might seek to influence.

Studs Terkel prefaced his bestseller, *Working* (New York: Pantheon Books, 1972), with the statement that:

> This book, being about work, is, by its very nature, about violence – to the spirit as well as to the body. It is about ulcers as well as accidents, about shouting matches as well as fistfights, about nervous breakdowns as well as kicking the dog around. It is, above all (or beneath all), about daily humiliations. To survive the day is triumph enough for all the walking wounded among the great many of us.

The founders of the Navvy Mission Society, the Christian Social Union, and the ICF leadership in 1920, especially Studdert Kennedy, would have recognised the truth of these words. They may well have been dismayed to discover that they were still being written 50 years after its first founding. It has been observed too, that the leaders and influencers of ICF, in the 1990s, became somewhat distanced from the realities of the shop floor.

John Weaver offers a parable from the life of a Baptist congregation in the English Midlands of the 1970s. A large influential church, with a packed Sunday morning family worship and a large number of young people at evening services is situated in a town of large shoe factories. In common with Baptist churches, decisions are taken in the church meeting, and the spiritual oversight of the church is in the hands of the minister and deacons. The diaconate is largely drawn from the owners and management of the shoe factories, while the congregation and church members are largely made up of the shoe workers. So, in church, as in work, the decisions and organisation of life is under the control of the powerful and those with influence.

Was there a danger for the ICF of the 1990s that it had fallen into a similar managerial captivity?

Chapter 8

Partnership in a new century

The Industrial Christian Fellowship (ICF) emerged into the twenty-first century as a very different organisation to the one that had been formed 80 years earlier; it had nothing like the scale of resources and connections that it once had, nor did it have any immediate expectation of becoming a major presence in mainstream society. However, it was a far more cohesive entity, achieved more than anything because of the relatively small number in its leadership and their common experience of seeing it through a period of significant uncertainty.

We might also reflect on the fact that, as a much smaller-scale operation, it was largely free to determine its own future and direction – those who might once have been concerned if its message strayed too far from their own, no longer considered it to wield sufficient power to cause them serious concern. The challenge of a new century was how to operate as a small organisation, albeit one with a remarkable history.

We have tried throughout this narrative to highlight key areas of reflection for those engaged in contemporary mission. One of those is to recognise when an organisation or project has run its course, and to test whether ongoing commitment is merely a loyalty to the institution itself or a genuine commitment to a definitive vision that remains relevant and necessary. These were questions that the newly formed Executive needed to ask itself, while also recognising that this now needed to be worked out in a very different world.

This included a growing realisation of the need to work in partnership, partly out of the necessity of ICF's own limited scale, but also because this approach very much epitomised the environment in which it now sought to operate. Yet as it explored that environment, genuinely acknowledging that its ongoing presence should not be taken for granted, the Executive concluded that no other organisation quite represented its defining vision in the way that ICF still did. Its key task was to articulate that vision within the broader conversations around mission and ministry that were fervently taking place in this new millennium.

In many respects, ICF faced the same challenges that confront any relatively small organisation with a big vision – how can it fulfil its purpose with relatively few resources? There were lessons to be learnt from its history. One of the eras in which it was most able to express the breadth and reality of what it stood for was in the days of the Navvy Mission. Within that context, the Mission was able to embody an expression of Christianity that genuinely defined and shaped the working lives of its followers and the community that formed around them. The Mission managed to embrace roles that in the decades which followed have been undertaken by those such as the trade unions, health and safety commissions, employers' groups, churches, missionary societies, local authorities and the welfare state. The Mission provided publications, libraries, schools, adult education, worship services, Sunday schools and much more. The reality of its impact is captured in Dick Sullivan's history of navvies: 'most people on public works were Christian, in a confused, non-sectarian way, in the end. Navvies were Christianised if not churched.'

Perhaps one reason the Mission was able to achieve this was because it was working in a sector of society that attracted less public interest than what might be described as the higher levels of the social strata, but it was also because it was able to focus its efforts in one clearly defined context. What Sullivan describes as a 'confused ... Christianity' might be expressed by ICF today as a Christian faith lived out in the world of work and commerce, rather than within the recognised institutions of the Church. In many respects, the Navvy Mission stands as an example of what ICF has sought to achieve across the whole of society ever since, particularly through seeking to exemplify its mission vision through the world of work. One of the questions that the newly formed Executive sought to grapple with as the early years of the new century took their course, was whether similar contexts and opportunities existed where it could focus its endeavours to again develop a tangible expression of what it stood for.

But another aspect of that uniqueness was that, at a crucial moment in its history, it sought to combine the on-the-ground endeavours of the Navvy Mission with intellectual concerns about how and why the conditions that it worked hard to overcome existed in the first place. As we have already observed, this was the dimension that the Christian Social Union (CSU) brought to its work. The twenty-first century was one where terms like 'gatekeeper' and 'influencer' became increasingly common, recognising that social change is often achieved not so much by forming a large and formidable organisation, but by bringing a compelling vision to the attention of the right people at the right time. For all that its membership had significantly declined, the newly formed Executive recognised that within its ranks there remained a number of key individuals in their fields; individuals who remained attracted by its vision and purpose. The way forward was to find those contexts where the effect of ICF's thinking could be demonstrated, and to seek those opportunities where its message could influence the actions and intent of those with the potential to be agents of change in a wider sphere. This was articulated in a later publication by Phil Jump, through a formative article entitled '21st Century Prophets'. In it, he outlined how the Church's reaction to contemporary issues is often to form some kind of think-tank or working group so that the Church in turn can develop its own response. Instead, he argued for an approach that developed the key theological narratives that represented a Christian perspective, and that the Church should seek to work outside of its own structures, to support leading experts and activists to become a 'prophetic voice', irrespective of their faith allegiances.

There were no immediate dramatic changes but, in the 20 years that followed, leading to ICF's centenary in 2020, a number of important developments took place. These are the focus of this final chapter.

Teams in the twenty-first century

The number of people directly involved in the Fellowship was now small, but there was a strong sense of team-work among the group who sought to take the organisation forward. All those involved were volunteers. Commitment by the Executive Committee was evident, with imaginative efforts being made to engage with many issues of faith and work. The partnership with the Ridley Hall Foundation (later Faith in Business) in the production of the *Faith in Business Quarterly* remained significant throughout. Although that partnership was particularly close, ICF was active in other partnering relationships.

The organisation was still having to adjust to the situation in which there were no paid staff. The core team was the Executive (whose members were also trustees), but taking forward the vision to 'influence the influencers', they also looked for support from others, especially the Council. Michael Fass took over from Geoffrey Brown as Chair of the Executive, with

Brown remaining involved through the Council. Carol Williams became the Executive's Vice-Chair. Bernard Weatherill had served as Chair of the Council for a decade and remained supportive, as did Anthony Loehnis, Frank Field and Peter Gardiner-Hill, who all knew the challenges ICF had faced in the 1990s. It had been customary throughout the Fellowship's history for the Archbishop of Canterbury to be its President, and this continued in the twenty-first century. However, when contact was made in 2001 with George Carey, who was coming towards the end of his time as Archbishop, it was clear that issues of faith and work were not current priorities. Nonetheless, when Rowan Williams succeeded Carey a year later, he accepted the position of ICF President.

An ICF conference held in 2002 at Ealing Abbey, hosted by Edmund Flood, had some of the characteristics of a team-building event. There was also a sense of renewed purpose in the Council in 2003, with the addition of new members: Lynne Sedgmore, a CEO who was interested in how spirituality could be integrated into leadership practices, Andrew Bradstock, who was National Secretary for Church and Society within the United Reformed Church, and Martin Wharton, Bishop of Newcastle. Changes on the Executive in 2003/04 were significant. John Lovatt stood down. He had made an enormous contribution, in administration, editorial work, handling publications and sales, producing liturgical material, and liaising with related organisations. Edmund Flood, who had brought wide experience of Roman Catholic involvement on both sides of the Atlantic in the field of faith and work, had also decided to retire.

As the composition of the two bodies began to settle, the Executive recognised the need for a clear development plan, and invited Phil Jump to act as facilitator for one of its early residential gatherings, which took place at Holland House near Pershore. Phil Jump was one of a cohort of newly appointed 'Regional Ministers' within the Baptist Union of Great Britain, specifically seeking to place people with a background in mission strategy in key regional roles. Before Baptist ministry he was a marine electrical engineer and worked for Cammell Laird Shipbuilders, where he became Material Control Manager. His working life had developed against the backdrop of computerisation within engineering design and logistics and he brought significant experience of strategic planning both in industry and more recently in community development. Phil had also worked with the Metropolitan Police as a Chaplain, as well as providing informal chaplaincy to local schools and healthcare workers through his community links. Phil helped the Executive to sharpen its vision into a defined strategic plan, and through that engagement was invited to join the Executive on a permanent basis.

Communication was a key element in that plan and another new Executive member, Paul Pearce, took on responsibility for making a website operational. This was an integral part of the new overall strategy. At the time, online publications were still a relatively novel feature, particularly in the charity and non-profit sector. The Executive recognised the communication potential it offered and sought to use its online presence to complement its printed publications and regular printed *Newsletter*. The *Newsletter* provided support and information to the wider ICF team – the members – through its articles, book reviews, theological 'jottings' and news of its own or other relevant initiatives, resources and events. In keeping with its vision to work in partnership, the *Newsletter*, and later the website, was able to make ICF members aware of relevant activities and initiatives from other faith and work organisations. One new move in this period was to hold Executive meetings in different parts of the country, with at least one a year being a 24-hour residential meeting. This was a response to the recognition that most of the regional networks had now dissolved, so it was difficult to physically bring members together without some being involved in significant travel. The different locations gave the Executive opportunities to connect with members locally and to hold seminars that were intended to attract others, thus promoting its work. There was a very clear focus in this period on the commitment to be defined as a membership organisation, seeking as much as possible to operate in ways that would attract new members. In 2005/06, residential meetings of the Executive were held in Southport, Salisbury and Newcastle-upon-Tyne, with an additional day meeting in Croydon. Much of the administrative work was undertaken by Ann Wright. She became Membership Secretary and later took on responsibility for ICF finances.

Although the ICF Council was able to attract new members – with further additions being Alistair Burt, a Conservative MP, and David Drew, a Labour MP – the Council did not strengthen the Fellowship's life as it was hoped. This was mainly because arrangements for meeting proved difficult. After a few years what had been an important body was put into abeyance. However, the appointment of two ICF Vice-Presidents was significant. These were Cardinal Cormac Murphy-O'Connor, Archbishop of Westminster, and David Coffey, Free Church Moderator. Together with Rowan Williams as President, this meant that the Fellowship was linked at the highest level with the main Christian traditions in England. The Executive remained a committed group with a membership of eight during the first decade of the twenty-first century. Executive members in this period who had longer-term ICF experience were Terry Drummond, Anthony King and John Raymond.

ICF had inherited a somewhat complex financial structure, a remnant from the days when its activities were on a far more ambitious scale. Despite his claims that he lacked the necessary financial skills, Anthony King took on the role of Treasurer and brought the finances into a far more manageable form, and restructured legacy investments to achieve a more regular income.

From 2004 to 2011, Carol Williams was Chair, the first woman in that position. Although these were no longer formalised, ICF's historical ties with the Church of England remained evident. In 2008, for example, it was delighted to endorse a motion passed by the Church of England's General Synod which affirmed work 'as essentially a spiritual activity' and which called for 'the engagement of the Church of England with the economic sector' to be examined.

In 2011, Phil Jump became Chair of the Executive, which represented another first: a Baptist as chair for the first time. The Annual Report for the year ending 31 March 2012 paid fulsome and deserved tribute to Carol Williams for 'steering the organisation through some difficult issues'. The expectation was of Phil Jump 'building a new team to take the Fellowship forward'. The challenges that were noted included 'exploring strategic partnerships with appropriate organisations with an interest in faith and work, and finding new ways to fulfil ICF's purpose and focus – to relate Christian faith to life in the workplace – in the ever-changing world of work.' The 'new team' was at most five Executive members. Phil's networks certainly brought a Baptist presence to the Executive. In 2012, continuing members included Jeremy Brown, Regional Minister in the South West Baptist Association, whose background in accountancy made him a welcome successor to Anthony King. John Raymond was also welcomed back to the Executive for this period and continued to contribute through a number of pamphlets and articles. He also maintained a strong interest base through the Diocese of Peterborough, in which ICF was able to play and active role. Phil's work in the North West brought him into contact with Canon Mike Vincer, Chaplain to Manchester airport, with whom he collaborated to develop a chaplaincy course. When Mike retired from his role at the airport, he was persuaded to join the Executive, though sadly his term of service was relatively short because of ill health. That year also saw the addition to the Executive of Dave Law, an industrial chemist who had played a key role in the development of 'Reading at Work', a faith and work network based in the Berkshire town, and also brought experience of working with social media. Much imaginative effort was expended in the years that followed, but despite all of this, ICF membership continued to decline year by year. In 2017, the Executive comprised Phil Jump, Dave Law, Andrew Bradstock and John Weaver, a theologian, who researched in the dialogue between science and faith, with a background in structural geology and former Principal of the South Wales Baptist College. Also in 2017, individual ICF membership fell below 100.

Imaginative efforts

Recognising its limitations, ICF had sought to particularly identify specific aspects and experiences of work where its vision could be exemplified, especially those which were emerging. In the early meetings at Holland House, some initial thought centred around the growing incidence of casual home working, and particularly issues of justice and isolation that emerged from that. The capacity to pursue this was never found, though with hindsight the Fellowship could claim to have had some early instinct of more recent concerns that have centred around what has come to be called the gig economy. Throughout this period, it maintained this focus of seeking to discern priorities and then move to implementation. Members were drawn into this by means of a questionnaire. The Executive was pleased with the quality and quantity of the 102 responses received. Many questions had been deliberately open-ended, and these had provided helpful suggestions. Much of the collation and presentation of these was again due to the quiet endeavours of Anthony King. It was clear that a key issue was how individuals faced problems and changing situations in their work. Although some mentioned help and support from their local church, a cause of much concern was that many churches did not seem to be taking issues of faith and work seriously enough. It was generally regarded as positive, however, that people appeared to be more interested in individual spirituality and corporate responsibility at work than they were a few years previously. The survey recognised that clergy and ministers had a role to play in responding to this development, but the best route to reaching people at work did not appear to be through the bishops or higher levels of clergy. There was a call for ICF to think more clearly about what it could offer to support and train those in the workplace. It seemed right to look at what was described as 'ICF's unique traditions of lay ministry and deep theological reflection', in order to affirm, in a relevant way, 'Christ the Lord of all Life'.

Under the leadership of Carol Williams, the Executive gave attention to these issues. Out of this process, Executive members identified important features of the Fellowship's vision and agreed on the three that were seen as the most significant. These were summarised as a combination of practical experience and theological reflection, an understanding of the need to equip lay people for their ministry, and a tradition of being prophetic and challenging. The ecumenical dimension was also stressed. This led to the formulation of a statement that affirmed ICF's purpose:

> to support and equip God's people for their ministry and vocation in secular work. It does this by its unique combination of theological reflection on faith/work issues, networking with other organisations and the publication of worship and other relevant material. It is a broad-based, national, ecumenical organisation, working alongside established Church structures. Throughout its history it has retained the ability to act flexibly, move with the times and speak with a prophetic and challenging voice on issues concerning faith and work.

The Executive agreed that, without a physical office, there was a need for the Fellowship to become 'more light-footed and flexible'. There were reserves of around £60,000, and it would seek as much as possible to use these only for strategic projects while covering its operating costs from revenue income.

In 2003, ICF achieved considerable press coverage through a headline, 'Pray for stockbrokers and accountants'. The statement highlighted a lack of prayer in churches for those who were working in the banking and finance sectors, seeking to place some of the core messages of the previous century's theme pamphlets into the public domain. The hope was that a campaign could gather momentum which would result in congregations broadening Sunday service prayer slots by including prayers for people in the financial service and manufacturing sectors. A report had found that most churches focused almost entirely on the clergy and the 'caring' professions – teachers, nurses, social workers – when they included 'workers' in their intercessions. The ICF statement concluded:

> We need an increased awareness and acceptance by clergy and laity that work is part of God's creation and Christians need to be supported and equipped to live out their faith in their lives. Once you include accounting or fund-managing in intercessions, it underlines the fact that these careers are all part of God's world.

As a follow-up, ICF highlighted liturgy and prayer resources it provided, and requests for this material were received from a number of non-ICF members. We can only speculate on how various behaviours and scandals that emerged a few years later might have been affected if ICF's call to prayer had been more fully heeded!

This though was a steep learning curve. In reality, the success of the press campaign (achieved through the endeavours of a freelance press officer) revealed a lack of capacity to follow this up. Although no future campaign has ever achieved the same reach, they were undertaken with considerably more appreciation of what was involved, and with a greater readiness to offer a more tangible response to enquirers.

Annual Lectures continued to function as opportunities to communicate. In 2003, Nigel Wright, Principal of Spurgeon's College and President of the Baptist Union, spoke on 'Participating without Possessing: The Public and Private in Christian Discipleship'. A year later Canon Robert Wright, Chaplain to the Speaker of the House of Commons, took the topic 'God in Governance'. In the following year the lecture, on 'Prosperity with a purpose: Mission in the Public Arena', was given by Tom Butler, Bishop of Southwark. The 2006 lecture, by Canon John Atherton, was entitled, 'The Happiness Hypothesis: Reflections from the Religion and Capitalism Debate', addressing issues that were being raised by political and religious organisations. In 2007, the venue for the lecture was Portcullis House, London, arranged by Alistair Burt MP, with Professor Hilary Russell speaking on 'Building on Rock or Sand: Reflections on the Language and Dilemmas of Regeneration', giving an overview of changes in government policy on community regeneration. She highlighted challenges and opportunities presented to faith communities. Colin Hicks, former Director General of the British National Space Centre, gave the 2008 lecture, on 'The Universe of Christ', offering insights into the wonders of creation and the moral issues presented by new technology. The last lecture of this decade was by Ruby Beech, Director of Corporate Services for Hestia Housing and Support, on 'Equal Opportunities: Political Correctness Gone Mad or a Gospel Imperative?' The lectures during the decade showed the quality of speakers that ICF could still attract.

Publications, too, remained an important channel of communication. One influential book was *Faith in Governance: Renewing the role of the Director* by Michael Fass and Michael Willis, and another was Julian Reindorp's *Equipping Christians at Work*, which was sponsored and marketed by ICF. It sold 1,000 copies, which covered costs. A number of pamphlets were issued in the period 2000–2009, including several that issued from Annual Lectures. Others were *The Balancing Act*, on work–life balance, edited by Denis Claringbull, and a booklet on lay discipleship by Carol Williams, *Putting Faith to Work*. Prayer cards were issued and were popular. The main means of communication with ICF members was the *Newsletter*, with three issues each year. Phil Jump took on editing the *Newsletter*. It was updated and redesigned, with greater use of colour and illustration. Each issue had a theme. For example in 2007 the three topics were: 'The Cross Factor: Does being a Christian really make a difference in the workplace?'; 'Faith on the High Street – Reflecting on the growing place of ethics in consumer preferences'; and 'Embracing Europe: Often presented as a political sideshow, is this a defining issue for Christians in the next decade?' It might not have been 'defining'; it was certainly to prove deeply divisive.

Faith in Business Quarterly

By 2007, the *Faith in Business Quarterly* had been produced for ten years. It had become a well-respected vehicle supporting the widespread concern for 'thinking Christianly' about business and professional issues. The Executive was pleased to note the success of the partnership with a growing circulation that had increased beyond the break-even point. It was considered that the quality of the journal represented a good return on the significant financial contribution that ICF had made, and involvement was also represented editorially. John Lovatt was a long-lasting editor, along with Richard Higginson. Lovatt was joined by Carol Williams, and Anthony King served on the journal's steering group. The group was chaired for several years by Clive Wright. In the three years up to 2007, topics examined in *FiBQ* included capitalism; the Sabbath; trade justice; leadership; taxation; social enterprise; philanthropy; the modern credit economy; economic empowerment; micro unions; the role of supermarkets and small businesses; daily work and the Eucharist; Catholic social teaching in the market economy; the impact of climate change on business; manufacturing ethics; and executive pay and corporate governance.

Over succeeding years, this presence was maintained. Canon David Driscoll joined the ICF Executive and became part of the *FiBQ* editorial team. In his early period of involvement, the journal examined the background paper for the Church of England's General Synod debate on faith, work and economic life. It also looked at economic theories and practical implications of the financial crisis of 2006 to 2008. Richard Higginson was both Director of Faith in Business and a greatly valued *FiBQ* editor. Other journal editors came from the Faith in Business network, such as Sally Orwin Lee, a consultant in change and development. Coverage of the change and challenge that issued from the financial crisis continued to feature in *FiBQ*, with articles appearing on, for example, 'Thrift, magnanimity and magnificence as positive routes out of the economic crisis'; 'The corporate accountability debate, social responsibility and banking'; and 'Redundancy, work, suffering and stress'.

In the second decade of the twenty-first century, the journal continued to cover major issues such as sustainability, ethics in business, and inequality. David Driscoll stood down, and his place was taken by Fiona Stewart-Darling, Bishop's Chaplain to the Docklands. She also gave the ICF Annual Lecture in 2011, held at Bloomsbury Baptist Church, on 'The Human Face of Banking'. John Lovatt continued to serve on the editorial team during the whole of this period. New features in this period included interviews with Christians in business and a regular 'ICF page', which raised the profile of the Fellowship beyond the membership.

Phil Jump was struggling to produce a regular newsletter along with other responsibilities, so during this time it was decided to focus instead on developing online resources, and for him to also play a fuller role in writing material for *FiBQ*. He began to provide a regular full-page article, seeking to retain ICF's approach of commenting on topics of current interest. When Stewart-Darling brought her period with *FiBQ* to an end, John Weaver took over on the editorial board. One of Weaver's particular concerns was the impact of climate change and he wrote and spoke extensively on this topic.

John Weaver handed over his role to Anthony Harrop, who brought extensive expertise as a Senior Publishing Consultant with the United Bible Societies. In April 2016, Harrop attended what had become an influential annual event, the Faith in Business Conference in Cambridge and in 2018 John Lovatt attended, as he had done on some previous occasions. ICF's partnership with Faith in Business, through the *Quarterly*, was of considerable importance, since *FiBQ* had become known as a leading contributor to contemporary thinking on faith and work. In 2017, the ICF Executive spoke about the forthcoming retirement of Richard Higginson from his posts as Director of Studies, Tutor in Ethics and Director of Faith in Business at Ridley Hall. The Executive noted with great pleasure that he would continue to act as lead editor of *FiBQ*. The links between ICF and Faith in Business remained strong. A revised version of Karen Blakeley's ICF Lecture from 2017 on 'Leadership, Love and the Transformation of Business' was included in the journal. With Richard Higginson's retirement, Peter Heslam was appointed as the new Director of Faith in Business. He had been the Director of a research project of the London Institute for Contemporary Christianity (LICC) on a Christian response to contemporary capitalism. LICC, under its Director Mark Greene, became another partner on issues of faith and work. Heslam took on organising the annual Faith in Business Conference. Anthony Harrop attended in 2019 and spoke of the inspiration and refreshment the event provided.

Collaboration

Although the partnership with *FiBQ* was particularly close, throughout this period ICF was also active in building links and working co-operatively with other organisations. The most notable were the Christian Association of Business Executives (CABE), MODEM, the Peterborough 'People and Work' programme, Christians in Secular Ministry (CHRISM) and EBEN (European Business Ethics). Geoffrey Brown was also involved in CABE and he was a strong advocate of partnership. Through working together, these organisations were able to put on events that would have been difficult for a single organisation to arrange. An example was the CABE-initiated annual Hugh Kay Memorial Lecture. In 2001 Rowan Williams, then Archbishop of Wales, gave this lecture. His topic was 'Ethics and Globalisation'. The venue was St Botolph's Aldgate in London. About 150 came to what was considered a very successful event. Speakers at subsequent Hugh Kay lectures included Sir Mark Moody-Stuart, Chair of Anglo American plc, and a former Chairman of Shell, on 'The Role of Business in Developing Countries', and James Jones, Bishop of Liverpool, on 'Must Business Cost the Earth?' Growing co-operation also developed with the Industrial Mission Association and a number of its regional groups. Phil Jump and Carol Williams led seminars at its national conference and chaplains' away days for the Black Country Industrial Mission and Military Chaplains, an opportunity to again recognise the legacy of Studdert Kennedy.

Throughout much of its history, ICF had not been as closely associated with Evangelical Anglicans as with other Anglican streams, although Evangelicals had been involved. In the twenty-first century, relationships with Evangelicals in the Church of England, as well as in other denominations, came much more to the fore. The link with Ridley Hall was part of this, since Ridley was a leading college representing open evangelicalism. The 'openness' included learning from varied Christian traditions. Thus, in 2001, a Ridley Hall Foundation conference on spirituality and the workplace featured as main speakers Richard Higginson and Graham Cray, the former Principal who was now Bishop of Maidstone, and also speakers such as ICF's David Welbourn and Angela Tilby, Vice-Principal of Westcott House, Cambridge. Among ICF's other Evangelical connections were Christians at Work (previously the Workers' Christian Fellowship) and Spring Harvest, which in 2002 put on an event, 'At Work Together', with 1,000 people attending. John Weaver attended all four weeks of Spring Harvest in 2018, speaking on 'Discipleship in a Time of Climate Change'.

Through what soon became known as the 'Collaboration Group' of organisations, the Fellowship became involved in events at St Paul's Cathedral hosted by the St Paul's Institute. The relationship with the Institute developed over the two decades. With other members of the Collaboration Group, ICF exhibited at the Greenbelt Christian Arts Festival held annually at Cheltenham. This became an annual undertaking. Carol Williams, who acted as the ICF representative on the Collaboration Group, also forged links with Telos, a Church in Wales initiative 'to contribute to the transformation of Wales … and develop a new understanding of the meaning of work and spirituality in organisational culture'. In 2005, she and Ann Wright attended the Anglican Adult Education Network conference, 'Resourcing a Living Faith', and took part in a 'marketplace' session and panel discussion. There were also connections with the Industrial Mission Association and the European Christian Industrial Movement (ECIM). When the European movement came to an end, its assets were transferred to ICF.

New networking possibilities emerged throughout this period. One new relationship was with SCORE (Sports Chaplains Offering Resources and Encouragement), which supported and resourced a network of over 170 chaplains in all aspects of sport. In 2008, ICF began supporting Mary Vickers in her role as Co-ordinator for chaplaincy for women in sport. Another connection that was made was with Mission in London's Economy (MiLE), which launched a report on faith and work, focusing particularly on chaplaincy, in 2010. ICF contributed to the research for the report. The research paper led to a discussion at the Merseyside Mission in the Economy (MitE) where Phil Jump was invited to bring an ICF perspective on the issues raised. In the same period the Church of England's General Synod received a report on faith and work. ICF supported this with a special print run of resources and Ann Wright co-ordinated its presence at the event.

ICF built on existing relationships with the Free Churches. In 2011, Carol Williams represented the Fellowship at a Methodist Diaconal Order for Faith and Work consultation in Birmingham on the Kingdom at Work project. Cambridge was the venue for an event in 2014 hosted by Paul Hills, Eastern Baptist Association Regional Minister, under the title 'Faith that Works on Monday'. John Weaver spoke about Christian responsibility in the face of increasing intense climate events; Dorothy Peyton Jones of People at Work spoke about the difference that chaplaincy makes in work situations; and Phil Jump gave a presentation on 'Dark, Satanic Mills: When Christian action by working people changed history'. These presentations were videoed and made available through the ICF website. Free Church interest continued, with Phil Jump writing in the *Methodist Recorder* on justice and holiness, linking with ICF's interest in workplace justice and writing a series of home group studies for the Joint Public Issues Team (Baptist, Methodist and United Reformed Church) for publication in 2017. Another Baptist link was that Lynne Green, General Secretary of the Baptist Union, became Vice-President of ICF.

ICF-linked lectures, seminars and events held in different parts of the country also offered opportunities for networking. A lecture was convened in Liverpool in 2009 at which Professor Hilmar Warenius FRCP, former head of Liverpool University's Department of Oncology and founder of leading research group TheRyte, was the guest speaker. He gave insights into his work in searching for a cure for cancer and made clear the way in which his working life and faith were integrated. On another occasion, in the following year, Professor Ian Arbon of Glasgow University made an effective presentation on sustainability and ethics. The Executive felt this should be published. In the North West of England, ICF played a particularly active role in the development of the 'Salt of the Earth' network, an initiative originally set up by the Bishop of Birkenhead, seeking to celebrate the industrial heritage of the Cheshire salt and chemical industry, and to foster community, church and business relationships. Phil Jump became a member of the steering group, and in 2015 John Weaver was invited to speak at Salt of the Earth gatherings on fracking, science and faith. Those attending included two bishops and two senior directors of firms involved in fracking. Weaver's perspectives on the issues were appreciated, once again reflecting ICF's heritage of bringing together opposing opinions to explore areas of common ground. In the South East, Dave Law, based in Reading, ran 'Reading at Work', which led to similar creative partnerships. As with Salt of the Earth, while ICF struggled to sustain groups of this nature on its own, it was able to 'add value' to local initiatives through financial and practical support. The 2017 Annual Lecture, given by Karen Blakeley, Senior Lecturer in Human Resources and Management and Head of the Centre for Responsible Management at Winchester Business School, opened conversations with the Centre for Theology and Religion in Public Life at Winchester University. Collaboration had become central to ICF life.

The breadth and effectiveness of these partnerships is a testimony to the ongoing significance of ICF's founding vision. Although no longer a major player, the Fellowship was able to show itself to be flexible and light on its feet. One example of this was its participation in Liverpool's International Business Festivals in 2014 and 2018. On both occasions, the local faith community had been able to secure a significant presence, again through collaboration between key agencies, especially MitE and Churches Together in Merseyside, of which Phil Jump was Vice Chair. On the first occasion, as proceedings got under way, faith groups recognised that they were struggling to communicate their message at the core of the event. ICF was able to design and produce the resource 'What's Faith Got to do With It? – 10 reasons why your business should take faith seriously' in less than a week. In 2018, after being provided with somewhat unsuitable meeting space, ICF was able to commission and provide a set of banners, which not only promoted the cause of faith and work but also enabled the space to be more appropriately defined. Again, a small Executive and lighter organisation was able to respond quickly and effectively at a moment of need.

Research, resources and relationships
In 2010, the Executive recognised the need to revisit and refresh its development plan, which resulted in a significant presentation at its Annual General Meeting in November of that year. It set out a future direction that proposed three key activities. These were summarised by the trustees as 'three Rs'. The first of these was **research**: to build up a body of knowledge to inform ICF's work. This was sometimes referred to as increasing knowledge. Secondly there was a focus on **resources**: to equip ICF members and others to be able to consider the faith issues presented by economic life. Thirdly, it would continue to stress **relationships**, and would support ICF members in this important area of their faith. It would also remain committed to fostering partnerships with others with similar aims.

A crucial way in which ICF saw itself as contributing to relevant areas of research was through a programme of Fellowships. In the period 2010 to 2020, several of these were offered. It was not always possible for Fellowships to be taken up. Justin Welby, then Dean of Liverpool Cathedral, was invited to look at the implications of Christian social teaching for the exit from the financial crisis. He was not able to pursue this as he became Bishop of Durham, but he reconnected with ICF as its President after he became Archbishop of Canterbury. Fellowships were awarded to Ian Arbon, to publish an essay bringing out the research he had done on sustainability and ethics, to Tim Presswood, to develop his thinking on alternative monetary systems, and to Andrew Drury who was looking at the way in which stress from the current economic situation was affecting work–life balance. Tim Presswood's Fellowship also ended with a presentation he gave on alternative currencies in July 2013. Andrew Drury's Fellowship was completed with the publication of the pamphlet, *What Recession? Exploring the personal impact of economic crisis.*

The work being undertaken by Ian Arbon took more time than some of the other research projects. He gave an update to the Executive in 2012. John Weaver provided theological perspectives and gave his expertise as an editor to bring this to publication. The resulting booklet, *Sustainability and Ethics*, published in 2014, was promoted through ICF and the John Ray Initiative (JRI), of which Weaver was, at the time, Chair. JRI, an educational charity bringing together scientific and Christian understandings of the environment, had a mission to promote responsible environmental stewardship in accordance with Christian principles and the wise use of science and technology. *Sustainability and Ethics* sold well at conferences, with additional publicity provided when it was mentioned in the *Church Times.* Further Fellowships were offered. *Workplace Spirituality: Does business have a soul?* was printed in 2017. Written by Andy Freeman, Co-Director and Founder of Space to Breathe, this discussion paper explored the way in which spiritual wellbeing had become an increasing priority for employers, in recognition of the impact of work on every aspect of personhood.

ICF had a long history of producing resources and, in keeping with the plan of 2010, this remained a focus. Pamphlets continued to be produced, in some cases arising from Annual Lectures, for example those given by Nigel Wright, Tom Butler and (in 2012) by John Devine. The 2012 lecture was on 'Finding a Voice for Faith: Reflections on engagement in the public square'. ICF also produced a book, *The Big Society: Ten questions for churches*, written by Phil Jump. It addressed what was a growing debate about the needs and challenges of Britain's communities and the Church's place within them. This was perhaps the nearest the Fellowship came to recreating the role it had had in the years after the wars. The 'Big Society' was heralded as a key platform of the incoming Government's social policy, and ICF sought to provide a significant publication to enable churches to engage. Sadly, the incoming administration's enthusiasm for this agenda was never matched with serious action or policy, and much of this endeavour proved largely wasted. Although the publication offers useful insights into church and community engagement, its particular emphasis made it appear obsolete.

The members' questionnaire some years earlier had identified the key role that local clergy had in supporting congregational members in the workplace. In response to this, ICF explored what contribution it might make to ministerial formation and training, to seek to provide better support for ministers and priests in this role. Initial discussions took place with a number of academic institutions, and eventually a partnership was formed with Lampeter college to pursue this further. The project was initiated by Carol Williams and then developed by Eric Forshaw. Sadly, because of his deteriorating health, although the basic work was completed, he was not able to take it forward to implementation. The Executive initially asked John Weaver, recently retired principal at South Wales Baptist College to take this work forward, an initial contact that led to John becoming a member of the Executive itself. As John reflected on the content of the programme, and the changing realities of ministerial training, he suggested that this might be better if it were recast as a resource for study groups in local churches. This was completed for publication in 2017 under the new title of 'Faith, Work and Christian Discipleship'. It was a series of six study outlines and a leader's guide under ICF's new branding of 'Living it out on Monday'. The aim was to help those in various forms of employment – paid and unpaid, employers and employees, volunteers, producers, carers, creators, customers, clients, managers and citizens – to consider how they might engage in these activities as faithful followers of Jesus.

Although ICF still valued printed material, there was a gradual move in this period to a greater focus on web-based resources. The website was seen as vital. It featured, for example, monthly 'lectionary prompts' which were appreciated by those preparing sermons and talks. Alongside such regular features, there were occasional reflections on current issues, and more personal devotional reflections for the working day. Paul Pearce took responsibility initially for the website, and later handed over this role to Phil Jump. Over 10,000 pages were downloaded from the website in 2012. There was a monthly average of 470 visitors in 2014 and this has grown steadily since to over 1,000. Linked to the website, Dave Law created an ICF presence on Twitter and Facebook. In 2016, over half of the available bandwidth on the website was used each month, and there were regular spikes when a reflection on a particular topic of current interest was posted. Website updating continued, with webmasters being Laura Jump and then Mark Jump. In 2017, Karen Blakeley's Annual Lecture was posted on YouTube and the lecture a year later was live-streamed. Ram Gidoomal spoke on 'Am I My Brother's Keeper: Can business build a better world?' and argued passionately for trade justice. Many ICF resources could be ordered from the website, or through the Amazon Bookstore, set up by Dave Law.

In the area of relationships, there was a commitment to developing deeper connections not only with like-minded organisations in the field but also with local churches. There were examples of local churches devoting time to looking at faith and work. St Andrew's in Histon near Cambridge was one, with a series of Sunday evenings entitled the 'World at Work', which attracted 60 to 80 people. ICF later developed an initiative called 'Take your Minister to Work'. This was envisaged as a partnership between local churches and their surrounding working communities to create an opportunity for serving clergy to engage with local employers and achieve a greater appreciation of the working lives of their congregations. It was particularly promoted in the season of Rogationtide and was featured on local radio in 2008. Two years later it was given publicity at a 'Joy of Work' conference in the North West. Over time, the project raised issues for communities and churches. It led to fruitful discussions and gave credibility to local initiatives to link faith and work. It was noted, however, that although it was generally well received by those in business and industry, engagement with clergy proved more difficult. This was an ongoing concern.

Looking to the future

As the second decade of the new century continued, the Executive recognised two key anniversaries that were on the horizon. The first was the centenary of the outbreak and then ending of the First World War, and the second was the centenary of the formation of ICF itself in the years immediately afterwards. The Executive was aware of the role that Studdert Kennedy had played within both that conflict and ICF's own history, and was keen to recognise this important relationship with the past. It was keen to re-present the work of Studdert Kennedy in a more contemporary context and, recognising his power as an orator, felt that being able to recapture his writings and poetry in a more 'performed' style might draw out their true power and significance. It was while researching for this that they stumbled across Searchlight Theatre Company, forging yet another significant partnership. Searchlight had already produced a play based on Studdert Kennedy's life which was due to be presented at the Edinburgh Fringe. David Robinson played the part of Studdert Kennedy in a way which brought this legendary figure to life. The Executive worked with Searchlight to promote the play and two national tours took place. David also agreed to star in a series of short films for DVD which sought, as much as possible, to follow word for word Studdert Kennedy's original writings. The pull-up banners and prayer cards prepared for the play were available afterwards for use by churches or groups and sales of the DVD continued to promote both ICF and the significance of Studdert Kennedy's thought and work.

Converting interest into membership, however, continued to be a challenge. At the end of 2018, the Fellowship had 75 individual members, 17 honorary members and two organisational memberships. Yet there was also some powerful encouragement in the same year. It was the 150th anniversary of the formation of the Trades Union Congress, and as part of the celebration of that milestone ICF's President, Justin Welby, addressed the annual TUC Congress. His participation was another reminder of ICF's history of involvement in management–union relationships. An article arising from this event was published on the website, which in turn led to a commission for a more reflective piece in the *Faith in Business Quarterly*. It was an opportunity to consider the formative role that ICF played in helping to forge vital connections between the emerging social justice agenda of trade unionists and others and the values and narratives of Christian faith and heritage.

The second anniversary was the formation of ICF itself, and it is at this point that this publication becomes part of the story. There were conflicting records about whether it was formed in 1919 or 1920. The research undertaken by Ian Randall explained this by indicating that it was in 1919 that the Navvy Mission changed its name to The Industrial Christian Fellowship, but it was not until 1920 that the partnership with the Christian Social Union was forged, creating the organisation as it then became. The trustees recognised that the future of ICF should not be taken for granted, but felt a shared responsibility that it should remain as an identifiable organisation to see its centenary through. They also felt that this was a time for its story to be told, so commissioned Ian Randall to begin the process of putting its story together. As the introduction indicates, the final text has been a much more collaborative affair, but owes its existence to Ian's significant endeavours.

Where ICF goes from here remains to be seen. Realism demands that, as another decade opens, this is acknowledged as the one in which this particular organisation may complete its course. If so, we offer this account of its story to say 'Well done, good and faithful servant', in the hope that it will inform and inspire others to take similar visions forward. But this is far from the only option, and this story has also been retold, as part of the current organisation's commitment to remind itself again of its core purpose, and to consider how this might yet help to define its way forward. Whatever outcomes eventually emerge, we offer this account of a heritage of sacrifice and vision that deserves to be celebrated and shared. Many of the eras of history it recounts, and the possibilities they spawned, are unlikely to ever be encountered in the same way again. But what will always remain, even beyond history itself, is the compelling truth that Jesus is the Lord of all life, and while that truth remains, there will always be a need for those who can convey it with imagination and purpose.

Conclusion

Those who seek to be faithful followers of Jesus are called to live a life that reflects this vocation in every aspect of their being. Much of that will be spent either in our own workplace or engaging in activities and places that are someone else's. Christian discipleship is described by Jesus as 'life to the full', so the way it impacts and is impacted by the world of work is significant.

The Industrial Christian Fellowship (ICF) and its predecessors the Navvy Mission Society (NMS) and the Christian Social Union (CSU) have always been concerned about the spiritual as well as the physical and mental aspects of those involved in the economic activity of a nation, which reflects the Christian emphasis on body, mind and spirit, worked out in holistic mission.

Christian spirituality may be understood as the way in which Christian individuals or groups aim to deepen their experience of God, or as Brother Lawrence (c.1614–1691) wrote, 'to practise the presence of God: the best rule of holy life.' The definition proposed by William Stringfellow in *The Politics of Spirituality* (Philadelphia: Westminster Press, 1984) is helpful:

> Whatever else may be affirmed about a spirituality which has a biblical precedent and style, spiritual maturity or spiritual fulfilment necessarily involves the whole person – body, mind and soul, place, relationships – in connection with the whole of creation throughout the era of time. Biblical spirituality encompasses the whole person in the totality of existence in the world, not some fragment or scrap or incident of a person.

The danger arises when we separate our body and mind from our spiritual being, which is a real possibility in the context of work, to the detriment of our whole person.

However, many Christians tend to live in two worlds: the private world of faith and the public world of work and daily life. To follow Christ in our daily lives involves asking God questions of each and every part of our lives. Bringing the private and public worlds together is the main task facing the Church as it seeks to engage with the whole of life in the mission of Christ. There can be a flight from reason, where worship becomes a welcome respite from a tough and demanding world, and we deny God the opportunity to encounter us in the concerns of our life in the world: to challenge, direct, forgive and bring peace.

In today's complex world, taken as a whole, religious faith can be a welcome oasis for people. It may be valued as an escape from the problems and demands which crowd in upon us from the media as well as from our working lives. Home and Church offer space to escape the confusion of a postmodern world. While Monday to Friday for most people is spent among the pressures and questions of a technological world with its pluralistic values and beliefs, Saturday can be spent in the safe space of home, and Sunday can offer a safe haven in Church. This division of our existence into sealed compartments can leave our working lives cut off from relationships with family and friends and disconnected from any spiritual foundation.

But we cannot live without meaning and purpose, and it is here that ICF has a continuing role, focusing on Christian faith in the workplace and in the life of all people. Christian discipleship is a full-time occupation, seven days a week, and Christian faith needs to relate to every part of our lives, for there is no part of our lives with which God is not involved. The Gospel teaches us that God is able to transform every part of our existence. The first sign in the Gospel according to John records Jesus transforming water into wine. For many readers of the Gospel, this has served as a metaphor of a faith that can transform our watery existence into the richness of the life redeemed through his blood.

An important aspect of the 'wholeness' of Christian spirituality is that we are able to relate what we believe to our personal experience. Our experience is informed by biblical and theological reflection, which is a central part of whole-life spirituality. Such spirituality emerges from a creative and dynamic synthesis of faith and life, which has to be worked out through a commitment to live out Christian discipleship actively, radically and with integrity.

The Emmaus road story (Luke 24:13–35), provides a powerful key to how our life and work experiences, good, bad and indifferent, can be turned around and become again for many a pathway with God towards the rewards of hope. For many people it is a long journey. It is a journey through experiences and places where God is close but may seem hidden. It is a journey away from the oppression we may feel in the light of other people's agendas. It is a journey away from ways of belief and faith which can no longer hold their trust in God. It is a journey that will offer resting places where Scripture will be re-examined through the eyes of Christ. It is a journey towards a new community of belief whose mission is defined by the grace and truth of God in Jesus.

Jesus on the road to Emmaus is a model of ministry and involvement in the mission of Christ today, of which the Navvy Mission and ICF missioners give good examples. Understanding people, sharing their lives, drawing on their own experience of life and of Christ's presence through his Spirit. These missioners knew the life of the workers, their questions, their joys and concerns, because they shared them. They were able to speak of how their faith in Christ, suffering with and for the world in love, had supported and strengthened their lives. This continues to be the challenge for those involved in relating faith in the workplace. At the heart of this ministry, we can place three questions for all our experiences: what does this say about God? What does it say about God's desire for each human life? And what does it say about the ways in which God works in the world?

Going back to the roots of ICF has been a valuable exercise as the vision and passion of those who brought it into existence will present the next generation with important lessons. However, we should not seek to replicate their actions, but rather recognise the principles by which they ministered and understood the mission of Christ in and for the world. The role of the members of ICF in this generation is to explore the ways in which the insights and prophetic ministry of the earliest missioners and messengers of ICF relate to the twenty-first-century workplace, and to take account of the endeavours of those with similar aspirations so as to work in a collaborative and complementary way.

It has been noted how spirituality is at the heart of the mission of ICF. Much of the CSU's thinking emerged from a conviction that at the heart of church-life was the Eucharist or Holy Communion, in which the bread and wine were channels of God's grace. The CSU passed a resolution that its members should be held together as the body of Christ, which was intended to commit them to social service. At one of the ICF clergy conferences in the 1930s, the social implications of the Eucharist were examined. It was agreed that this act of Christian worship could never be 'merely individualistic': it was essentially connected to Christian fellowship. Social evils such as slums, sweated labour and war were a breach of fellowship. At the beginning of the twenty-first century, *Faith in Business Quarterly* included an article on daily work and the Eucharist alongside others on topics such as capitalism, trade justice, social enterprise, the market economy and taxation.

Eleanor Kreider (*Communion Shapes Character,* Scottsdale: Herald Press, 1997, published in the UK as *Given For You: A Fresh Look at Communion*, Leicester: Apollos/IVP, 1998) suggests that one danger with our celebration of the Eucharist is that our view can become individualistic, narrow and small. She poses the question: how can we reclaim the piety of early Christianity in which the presence of the risen Lord, at his table, engaged the whole of the community's life – individual, social, and material – something the ICF clergy conference also addressed.

Each generation has found fresh insights from the New Testament communities. God, who is Spirit, reaches out to communicate with us through the bread and wine of the Supper. We receive forgiveness, joy, healing and reconciliation. The meaning of the cross is clearly seen as our worship proclaims the Lord's death, and Christ's own self-giving is mirrored in relationships within his Church. Kreider encourages churches to explore the themes of thanksgiving, feasting, sharing, reconciling, forgiving, healing, covenant, discipline, serving and justice. Such exploration shapes our individual characters and the character of the Church. The way we take communion makes a difference, for we act out or perform our Eucharistic theology. The language of ritual speaks most powerfully when it is deeply connected to the circumstances of people. In retelling the story of God's creating, redeeming and liberating love, we find that the Spirit is able to minister to our individual and community needs. So a commitment to acts of worship that continue to embrace rather than escape the broader realities of life is surely one focus for those who seek to follow the vision offered by ICF.

Our onward rush to so-called progress, where needs are fulfilled and demands grow, sees resources exhausted and pollution increase. Alongside this, we look for a theology of sustainability and recognise that this is part of the whole doctrine of creation. Covenant, with its themes of relationship, justice and sin, becomes the key underlying principle. The call of Christ is expressed as: 'Whoever wants to be my disciple must deny themselves and take up their cross and follow me' (Mark 8:34). This is a different sort of life, a Christ-like life, a life that is 'in Christ'. It is to deny self – to move away from a selfish materialistic lifestyle, to take up the cross-shaped life of sacrificial love – sharing God's good gifts of creation with all, and follow

Jesus – in his compassion for others and for the world. The call is to join in Christ's redemptive mission.

ICF has been in the vanguard of environmental concern. It is in the Malvern papers (1941) that we find some of the earliest recorded awareness of what would today be described as environmental issues, some 25 years before they appeared in scientific texts. It was not until the1970s that UK politics would recognise the significance of this agenda, when Edward Heath created the Department of the Environment in 1970, with the Secretary of State for the Environment as a cabinet position. The *ICF Quarterly* carried an article in 1970 by C. F. D Moule, Lady Margaret's Professor of Divinity at Cambridge, on the topic of humanity and nature in the New Testament. Moule argued for a biblical understanding of care for creation.

Today, as these issues have attracted the attention they deserve, it has highlighted the need to avoid the self-centred, individualistic ideas of happiness and consumption, where growth is seen as a virtue expressed in consumerism and personal satisfaction. We seek to plant seeds of transformation in the here and now – political, economic, ecological and societal seeds. ICF looks to continue presenting an alternative narrative, sovereignty and hope. Ian Arbon and John Weaver in *Sustainability and Ethics* (ICF, 2014) advocate competent 'PESTE' analyses in decision-making at corporate and government levels. It is important to consider the **p**olitical, **e**conomic, **s**ocietal, **t**echnological and **e**nvironmental aspects that affect such decisions. Arbon maintains that a sustainable future requires serious analysis, which must take account of the growth in global population and energy demand, as well as recognising climate change and the depletion of fossil fuels. Only by considering all of these aspects can truly sustainable and ethical solutions be found.

The MBA Oath, quoted in Arbon and Weaver, is a useful practical suggestion for an ethical and sustainable approach to business decision-making. It was developed by graduates of Harvard Business School's class of 2009 for graduating MBAs and current MBAs around the world. It is a voluntary pledge that seeks to create values that are responsible and ethical in business leaders, who are challenged to lead in the interests of the greater good. This oath encourages leaders to recognise their role in society to lead people and manage resources so as to create value that no single individual can create alone; and to make decisions that positively affect the wellbeing of people inside and outside their particular business enterprise, in the present and the future. Following this challenge leaders will refrain from corruption, unfair competition or business practices harmful to society.

They will protect the human rights and dignity of all people affected by their business enterprise, and will oppose discrimination and exploitation. They will protect the right of future generations to advance their standard of living and enjoy a healthy planet.

But, from a theological point of view, the 'bottom line' is that sustainable and ethical solutions will require a wisdom that is beyond that of human rationality. We need to be in tune with the wisdom of the creator of the universe and of human life. It is this wisdom that ICF seeks to offer to the world of work. This may seem to be beyond us but our ultimate hope is always in God. This is hope beyond the chaos and catastrophe of poor decisions of governments or corporations. It is a hope that includes accountability and judgement. This is hope in God, who is creator and redeemer, and who in love will ultimately make all things new.

In the Introduction we observed that Deuteronomy contains one of the most wide-ranging visions of a society that is defined by the goodness and justice of God. Its law-codes set themselves in direct contrast to the life of slavery and enforced labour from which the Israelite people had been liberated. In the book of Leviticus, we read that the inequalities of society were to be righted through the celebration of Jubilee (Leviticus 25), where the burdens of debt were to be cancelled, slaves set free and land returned to its original fair distribution among all the people. It is in these two Old Testament books that love of God and love for neighbour is first presented, and Jesus at the beginning of his ministry declared Jubilee (Luke 4:18–19).

At the wedding of Prince Harry and Meghan Markle in 2018, Bishop Michael Curry spoke passionately about the power of love. The source of this love is God (1 John 4:7, 12). The Bishop declared that there's power in love. There's power in love to help and heal when nothing else can. There's power in love to lift up and liberate when nothing else will. There's power in love to show us the way to live. He concluded his sermon with these words:

> When love is the way, then no child will go to bed hungry in this world ever again.
> When love is the way, we will let justice roll down like a mighty stream and righteousness like an ever-flowing brook.
> When love is the way, poverty will become history.
> When love is the way, the earth will be a sanctuary.
> When love is the way, we will lay down our swords and shields, down by the riverside, to study war no more.

When love is the way, there's plenty good room – plenty good room – for all of God's children. 'Cos when love is the way, we actually treat each other, well… like we are actually family.

When love is the way, we know that God is the source of us all, and we are brothers and sisters, children of God.

My brothers and sisters, that's a new heaven, a new earth, a new world, a new human family.

The ICF initiative Love:work, which was developed out of consultation with a number of local faith and work groups, seeks to commend a similar outlook within the workforce as a whole, by offering 'Ten Commandments for Christians at Work'. It seeks to express some key Christian values that might contribute to a healthy working environment.

These are:

1. **Be diligent** – remember that the main reason you are at work is because you have a job to do. Do it ethically and as well as you can – anything else you seek to be and do as a Christian in the workplace will be undermined if first and foremost you don't make this a priority. You may not be the best at your job, at times you might find it challenging and difficult, there may even be aspects of your work and workplace that you vehemently dislike. But have a reputation for always giving it your best shot; staying on task; for taking the job seriously; for being someone that others want to work with.

2. **Be alert** – to God's presence in your workplace and in the lives of those you work with. Recognise that God is present in your workplace as God is in every part of life. God shares with us the mundane or anxious moments, our successes and failures.

3. **Be forgiving** – and encourage others to forgive; be a peacemaker and a reconciler. As Christians we are those who are loved, accepted and redeemed by God, and God calls for us to work in reconciling the world to God. Through God's Spirit we work in God's redemptive mission for all humankind.

4. **Be caring** – look out for the wellbeing of those you work with. We live in God's world and God has called us to work in it and care for

it. So, in our work and in our workplace we should seek to operate with the wisdom and compassion of God, whose nature we share. Seek to understand and to empathise with your co-workers, who may have all sorts going on in their lives. Everyone is made in the image of God; everyone is loved by God; everyone is part of God's creation. Work as someone who God has commissioned to care for what he has made.

5. **Be honest** – with your time, and in what you say, even if at times your honesty is not popular. Do not go out of your way to criticise, but gain a reputation for being consistent in your words and deeds. Don't let your views and responses change depending on who is in the room. Be honest in how you use your employer's resources; be honest in your dealings with customers, clients and colleagues.

6. **Be healthy** and wholesome. We need to discover God's rhythm for life: of work and rest, busyness and reflection, labour and worship, vocation and prayer. Don't simply be sucked in by the cultures and narratives that prevail in the workplace, without holding on to your own sense of spiritual and physical wellbeing – allow a healthy life rhythm to define you and shape your attitudes and behaviours. Look after yourself – God made you; God loves you; your condition matters to God.

7. **Be prayerful** – pray for all those with whom you work, whether or not you get along with them. Each of them is a person who God loves and for whom Christ died. Remember that prayer involves listening to God; allocate time to intentionally seek God – what is God's purpose for your workplace? What are the needs and opportunities that work presents? How can you pray in response to them?

8. **Be generous** – recognise the pressures under which those with managerial responsibilities are operating. Seek to support them, encourage them and offer critical observations when these are truly needed. Help others out when they need it; be prepared to 'go the extra mile' – be kind and gracious when others appear to fail or you feel they have let you down.

9. **Be positive** – avoid harmful criticism, gossip and coarse or obscene language. Always behave in a courteous and morally correct way with those with whom you work. Take a positive attitude towards change and challenge. Be a sharer of hope.

10. **Be reliable** – do all you can to not let people down. If you say you will be there – be there; if you say you will do it – do it. If you are struggling or you know you can't do something – let people know, don't just 'disappear'. Plan your day and your life so there is room to cope with the unexpected. Don't be 'a clock-watcher' nor a time-keeper for others, rather demonstrate your life as a disciple of Christ, who is Lord of all workers and managers. Don't make promises you can't keep.

Whatever you do, do it all for the glory of God. (1 Cor 10:31)

The parallel themes of these ten commands with the Bishop's sermon and the MBA Oath give a framework for ICF's ministry to all in the working environment in the coming years.

Postscript

At 11.00 a.m. on 28 April 2020, as the writers of these chapters momentarily paused from their labours, Britain fell silent to observe a minute's silence to remember those health workers who had died during the Covid-19 pandemic. The commemoration was planned to coincide with International Workers Memorial Day, and the timing of 11.00 a.m. had an inevitable resonance with traditional remembrance events. It was organised as part of a collaboration between a number of public service trade unions including Unison, the Royal College of Nursing and the Royal College of Midwives. The initiative was utterly appropriate, and one that ICF would readily commend. It received widespread television coverage and was a truly moving moment. Many healthcare workers stood stoically in the forecourts and foyers of their places of work, proudly holding their union placards, with no strong political messages, simply expressing that sense of mutual solidarity on which trade unions were founded. In a number of settings healthcare chaplains led brief acts of reflection, though the media preferred to ignore these, rightly focusing instead on the workforce themselves, some of whom held the pictures or names of colleagues whose lives had been taken.

Observers of this event might easily argue that this simply underlines the fact that ICF is an organisation whose time has passed. Society does not need organised religion in order to honour those who have been lost with appropriate dignity and respect. There are other ways of communicating the reality that love has no greater expression than the laying down of one's life in service of others. And yet we might also remember that around 100 years earlier, ICF had been a staunch defender of the emerging trade union movement in the face of a society in which many viewed them with suspicion and disdain. We might also remember that many of the early architects of those trade unions were also leading figures in ICF, and through that fellowship were encouraged to see their involvement as a natural expression of their Christian faith. The remembrance event might instead be portrayed as a moment that revealed how those foundational Christian values have remained embedded, if unrecognised, in trade unionism ever since. Less than two years earlier, at the TUC's 150th anniversary, commentators had debated whether an Archbishop was right to take centre stage – now TUC members were organising vigils of remembrance. The ambiguity of that moment is that it could be described as an example of ICF's obsolescence, its hidden success or the vibrant necessity of its ongoing role. And so the task begins of working out which of these it is.

Selected further reading

Ian Arbon and John Weaver, *Sustainability and Ethics* (Industrial Christian Fellowship, 2014)

Andrew Chandler and David Hein, *Archbishop Fisher, 1945–1961* (Farnham: Ashgate, 2012)

David Clark, *Christians in Public Life* (Birmingham: Westhill College, 1992)

David Clark, *The Kingdom at Work Project: A communal approach to mission in the workplace* (Peterborough: Fast Print Publishing, 2014)

Dorothy Day, *Loaves and Fishes: The inspiring story of the Catholic Worker movement* (Maryknoll, NY: Orbis, 1963)

Albert M. Erisman, *The Accidental Executive. Lessons on Business, Faith and Calling from the Life of Joseph* (Peabody, MA: Hendrickson, 2015)

Faith in Business Quarterly

Michael Fass and Michael Willis, *Faith in Governance: Renewing the role of the Director* (Industrial Christian Fellowship, 2004)

Malcolm Grundy, *Unholy Conspiracy: Scandal of the Separation of Church and Industry Since the Reformation* (Norwich: Canterbury Press, 1992)

Richard Higginson, *Called to Account* (Guildford: Eagle, 1993)

Richard Higginson, *Faith, Hope & the Global Economy* (Leicester: IVP, 2012)

Richard Higginson, *Transforming Leadership: Christian Approach to Management* (London: SPCK, 1996)

Bob Holman, *Woodbine Willie: An Unsung Hero of World War One* (Oxford: Lion, 2013)

Margaret Kane, *Gospel in Industrial Society* (London: SCM-Canterbury Press, 1980)

John Kent, *William Temple: Church, State and Society in Britain, 1880–1950* (Cambridge: Cambridge University Press, 1993)

Eleanor Kreider, *Given for You: A Fresh Look at Communion* (Leicester: Apollos/IVP, 1998)

William Messenger, Theology of Work Project, *Calling and Work* (Peabody, MA: Hendrickson, 2015)

William Messenger, Theology of Work Project, *Theology of Work Bible Commentary*, Volumes covering the whole of the Bible (Peabody, MA: Hendrickson, 2015)

Linda Parker, *A Seeker After Truths: The Life and Times of G. A. Studdert Kennedy ('Woodbine Willie') 1883–1929* (Solihull: Helion & Co Ltd, 2018)

Linda Parker, *Shell-Shocked Prophets: Former Anglican Army Chaplains in Inter-war Britain* (Solihull: Helion & Co Ltd, 2015)

Julian Reindorp, *Equipping Christians at Work* (Industrial Christian Fellowship, 2000)

John W. Rogerson, *Industrial Mission in a Changing World* (Sheffield: Sheffield Academic Press, 1996)

Peter Sedgwick, *The Enterprise Culture* (London: SPCK, 1992)

Fiona Stewart-Darling, *Multifaith Chaplaincy in the Workplace. How Chaplains Can Support Organizations and their Employees* (London: Jessica Kingsley, 2017)

G. A. Studdert Kennedy, *Food for the Fed-Up* (Liskeard: Diggory Press, 2007)

G. A. Studdert Kennedy, with Thomas O'Loughlin and Stuart Bell (eds), *The Hardest Part: A Centenary*, Critical Edition (London: SCM, 2018)

G. A. Studdert Kennedy, *The Unutterable Beauty: The Collected Poems of G. A. Studdert-Kennedy ('Woodbine Willie')* (Liskeard: Diggory Press, 2006)

Gerald Studdert-Kennedy, *Dog-collar Democracy: The Industrial Christian Fellowship, 1919–1929* (London: Macmillan Press, 1982)

Dick Sullivan, *Navvyman* (London: Coracle Books, 1983)

John Weaver, *Outside-In. Theological Reflections on Life* (Oxford: Regent's Park College/Macon, GA: Smyth & Helwys, 2006)

Alan Wilkinson, *Christian Socialism: From Scott Holland to Tony Blair* (London: SCM, 2012)

Papers, booklets and contacts are available from the ICF website, www.icf-online.org